Mastering
the KITCHEN AID
STAND MIXER

Eloise Ford

To Esther, thank you for your support, enthusiasm, and love for cooking and baking.

I appreciate you always being there to taste, critique, and celebrate every dish.

Contents

Introduction v

1 Getting Started with Your Stand Mixer 6

2 Bread Baking 9

3 Cakes and Cupcakes 19

4 Cookies and Bars 29

5 Pastries and Pies 38

6 Savory Dishes 49

7 Whipping and Meringues 59

8 Doughs and Batters 67

Conclusion 74

Measurement Conversions 75

About the Author 766

Recipe Index 77

Introduction

For over a century, KitchenAid has been a trusted name in kitchen appliances, known for its commitment to quality, durability, and innovation. The KitchenAid Stand Mixer is a true testament to this legacy, beloved by professional chefs and home cooks alike for its reliability and versatility. From kneading dough to whipping cream, the stand mixer can handle a wide range of culinary tasks with ease, making it an indispensable companion in any kitchen.

The KitchenAid Stand Mixer is more than a luxury item—it's an investment in your cooking and baking endeavors. Its ability to mix, knead, whisk, and more with consistent results makes it an indispensable ally for a variety of recipes. This book will show you how to harness its capabilities to create everything from airy cakes to hearty breads, delicate pastries to savory dishes.

In the pages that follow, you will find a comprehensive collection of recipes organized by category, each designed to showcase the strengths of your stand mixer. I've included detailed instructions, helpful tips, and techniques to ensure success, whether you're preparing a simple batch of cookies or an elaborate layer cake.

So, roll up your sleeves, plug in your mixer, and let's get started on this exciting culinary adventure together!

Chapter 1: Getting Started with Your Stand Mixer

This chapter will guide you through the initial steps of setting up and using your stand mixer, ensuring you're ready to tackle any recipe with confidence. From unboxing to understanding the various attachments, you'll learn how to maximize the potential of this versatile kitchen appliance.

Unboxing and Setup

Unboxing Your Stand Mixer

- Carefully unpack your stand mixer, ensuring all components are present.
- Components typically include the stand mixer base, mixing bowl, and attachments (paddle, whisk, dough hook).

Setting Up Your Stand Mixer

1. Placement: Find a sturdy, flat surface near an electrical outlet for your stand mixer. Ensure it's in a convenient location for your kitchen workflow.
2. Attachment Installation:
   - Attach the mixing bowl to the base by aligning it with the bowl locks and twisting it into place.
   - Select the appropriate attachment (paddle, whisk, or dough hook) and attach it to the mixer head by inserting it into the attachment hub and turning it clockwise until it locks.

Key Attachments and Their Uses

Paddle Attachment (Flat Beater)

- Ideal for mixing normal to heavy batters.

- Uses: Cookie dough, cake batter, mashed potatoes.

Whisk Attachment

- Perfect for whipping air into ingredients.

- Uses: Whipped cream, meringues, frosting.

Dough Hook Attachment

- Designed for kneading yeast doughs.

- Uses: Bread dough, pizza dough, pasta dough.

Basic Techniques

Understanding Speed Settings

- Stir: Gentle mixing for starting dry ingredients or incorporating delicate ingredients.

- Speeds 2-4: Mixing and kneading doughs.

- Speeds 6-8: Beating, creaming, and medium-speed mixing.

- Speed 10: High-speed whipping and fast beating.

Proper Mixing Techniques

- Starting and Stopping: Always start at a low speed to avoid splattering. Gradually increase the speed as needed.
- Scraping the Bowl: Occasionally stop the mixer to scrape down the sides of the bowl with a spatula to ensure even mixing.
- Adding Ingredients: For best results, add ingredients gradually and follow the specific instructions in your recipe.

Getting Comfortable with Your Stand Mixer

Practice Makes Perfect

- Start with simple recipes to get comfortable with your stand mixer's capabilities and settings.
- Experiment with different attachments and techniques to discover how versatile your mixer can be.

Safety First

- Always unplug the mixer before changing attachments or cleaning it.

- Keep fingers and utensils away from moving parts while the mixer is in operation.

Maintenance Tips for Your KitchenAid Stand Mixer

1. **Regular Cleaning:** Clean the mixer after each use. Wipe down the body with a damp cloth and dry thoroughly. Wash the mixing bowl and attachments with warm, soapy water, and dry them before storing.

2. **Check for Wear:** Regularly inspect attachments and accessories for signs of wear or damage. Replace any worn-out parts to maintain the mixer's efficiency and safety.

3. **Lubricate Gears:** Some KitchenAid mixers require periodic lubrication of internal gears. Refer to the user manual for specific maintenance instructions or contact an authorized service center.

4. **Store Properly:** Store the mixer and its attachments in a dry, cool place. Avoid exposing the mixer to extreme temperatures or humidity.

5. **Avoid Overheating:** Allow the mixer to rest between heavy uses to prevent overheating. If the mixer becomes excessively hot, turn it off and let it cool down before resuming use.

6. **Secure Attachments:** Ensure that all attachments are securely fastened before use. Loose attachments can cause the mixer to malfunction.

7. **Check Power Cord:** Inspect the power cord regularly for any signs of damage. If the cord is frayed or damaged, do not use the mixer and have the cord replaced by an authorized technician.

8. **Service Regularly:** Schedule regular maintenance checks with an authorized KitchenAid service center to ensure your mixer remains in optimal working condition.

Chapter 2: Bread Baking

Bread baking is a timeless culinary art that transforms simple ingredients—flour, water, yeast, and salt—into a myriad of delicious loaves, rolls, and flatbreads. Understanding the fundamentals of bread making is key to achieving consistently good results. This chapter delves into the essential techniques and processes that form the foundation of bread baking.

Importance of Kneading

Kneading is a crucial step in bread making as it develops gluten, the network of proteins that gives bread its structure and texture. Gluten development ensures that the dough can hold the gases produced by the yeast, resulting in a light and airy loaf. Here's how to use your KitchenAid Stand Mixer to knead dough effectively:

1. **Initial Mixing:** Start by combining your ingredients in the mixer's bowl. Use the paddle attachment on a low speed to mix until the ingredients are roughly combined.
2. **Switch to the Dough Hook:** Once the ingredients are mixed, switch to the dough hook. This attachment is designed specifically for kneading and will do the heavy lifting for you.
3. **Kneading Process:** Begin kneading on a low to medium speed. The dough should come together and start to form a ball. Knead for 5-10 minutes until the dough is smooth, elastic, and slightly tacky to the touch.
4. **Windowpane Test:** To check if the dough is properly kneaded, perform the windowpane test. Stretch a small piece of dough between your fingers. If it forms a thin, translucent membrane without tearing, the gluten is well-developed.

Importance of Proofing

Proofing, or fermenting, is the period during which the dough rises. This step is essential for developing flavor and texture. Proper proofing allows the yeast to ferment the sugars in the dough, producing carbon dioxide gas that makes the dough rise.

1. **First Rise (Bulk Fermentation):** After kneading, place the dough in a lightly oiled bowl, cover it with a damp cloth or plastic wrap, and let it rise at room temperature. This process typically takes 1-2 hours, depending on the recipe and ambient temperature. The dough should double in size.
2. **Shaping:** Once the dough has completed its first rise, gently deflate it and shape it into loaves or rolls. Be careful not to overwork the dough during shaping, as this can expel the gas that has built up.
3. **Second Rise (Proofing):** After shaping, let the dough rise again. This second proofing is usually shorter, about 30 minutes to 1 hour. The dough should puff up and almost double in size again.
4. **Baking:** Preheat your oven before the second rise is complete. Baking times and temperatures will vary depending on the type of bread. Bake until the bread is golden brown and sounds hollow when tapped on the bottom.

Bread Baking Recipes

Classic White Bread

Servings: 1 loaf (12 slices)

Cooking Time: 3 hours (including rising time)

Ingredients:

- 2 1/4 tsp active dry yeast
- 1 1/4 cups warm water (110°F/45°C)
- 1 tbsp sugar
- 2 tbsp unsalted butter, melted
- 3 1/2 cups bread flour
- 1 tsp salt

Instructions:

1. In the mixing bowl, dissolve yeast in warm water with sugar. Let it sit for 5 minutes until frothy.
2. Add melted butter, 2 cups of flour, and salt. Attach the dough hook and mix on low speed until combined.
3. Gradually add remaining flour, 1/2 cup at a time, until dough forms and pulls away from the sides.
4. Knead on medium speed for 8 minutes until dough is smooth and elastic.
5. Place dough in a greased bowl, cover with a damp cloth, and let rise in a warm place for 1 hour or until doubled in size.
6. Punch down dough, shape into a loaf, and place in a greased loaf pan. Cover and let rise for another 30 minutes.
7. Preheat oven to 375°F (190°C). Bake for 30-35 minutes until golden brown and hollow sounding when tapped.
8. Cool on a wire rack before slicing.

Whole Wheat Bread

Servings: 1 loaf (12 slices)

Cooking Time: 3 hours (including rising time)

Ingredients:

- 2 1/4 tsp active dry yeast
- 1 1/4 cups warm water (110°F/45°C)
- 2 tbsp honey
- 3 cups whole wheat flour
- 1/4 cup vital wheat gluten
- 2 tbsp unsalted butter, melted
- 1 1/2 tsp salt

Instructions:

1. In the mixing bowl, dissolve yeast in warm water with honey. Let it sit for 5 minutes until frothy.
2. Add 1 1/2 cups flour, vital wheat gluten, melted butter, and salt. Attach the dough hook and mix on low speed until combined.
3. Gradually add remaining flour, 1/2 cup at a time, until dough forms and pulls away from the sides.
4. Knead on medium speed for 8-10 minutes until dough is smooth and elastic.
5. Place dough in a greased bowl, cover with a damp cloth, and let rise in a warm place for 1 hour or until doubled in size.
6. Punch down dough, shape into a loaf, and place in a greased loaf pan. Cover and let rise for another 30 minutes.

7. Preheat oven to 375°F (190°C). Bake for 30-35 minutes until golden brown and hollow sounding when tapped.
8. Cool on a wire rack before slicing.

Sourdough Bread

Servings: 1 loaf (12 slices)

Cooking Time: 24 hours (including fermentation time)

Ingredients:

• 1 cup active sourdough starter

• 1 1/2 cups warm water (110°F/45°C)

• 4 cups bread flour

• 2 tsp salt

Instructions:

1. In the mixing bowl, combine sourdough starter and warm water.
2. Add 3 cups flour and salt. Attach the dough hook and mix on low speed until combined.
3. Gradually add remaining flour, 1/2 cup at a time, until dough forms and pulls away from the sides.
4. Knead on medium speed for 10 minutes until dough is smooth and elastic.
5. Place dough in a greased bowl, cover with a damp cloth, and let rise in a warm place for 12 hours or overnight until doubled in size.
6. Punch down dough, shape into a round loaf, and place on a greased baking sheet. Cover and let rise for another 2 hours.
7. Preheat oven to 450°F (230°C). Bake for 30-35 minutes until golden brown and hollow sounding when tapped.
8. Cool on a wire rack before slicing.

French Baguette

Servings: 2 baguettes (16 slices)

Cooking Time: 4 hours (including rising time)

Ingredients:

• 2 1/4 tsp active dry yeast

• 1 1/2 cups warm water (110°F/45°C)

• 4 cups bread flour

• 2 tsp salt

Instructions:

1. In the mixing bowl, dissolve yeast in warm water. Let it sit for 5 minutes until frothy.
2. Add 2 cups flour and salt. Attach the dough hook and mix on low speed until combined.
3. Gradually add remaining flour, 1/2 cup at a time, until dough forms and pulls away from the sides.
4. Knead on medium speed for 8 minutes until dough is smooth and elastic.
5. Place dough in a greased bowl, cover with a damp cloth, and let rise in a warm place for 1 hour or until doubled in size.
6. Punch down dough, divide in half, and shape into baguettes. Place on a greased baking sheet, cover, and let rise for another hour.
7. Preheat oven to 450°F (230°C). Make diagonal slashes on the tops of the loaves.
8. Bake for 20-25 minutes until golden brown and hollow sounding when tapped.
9. Cool on a wire rack before slicing.

Brioche

Servings: 1 loaf (12 slices)

Cooking Time: 4 hours (including rising time)

Ingredients:

- 2 1/4 tsp active dry yeast
- 1/4 cup warm milk (110°F/45°C)
- 3 1/2 cups bread flour
- 1/4 cup sugar
- 1 tsp salt
- 4 large eggs
- 1 cup unsalted butter, softened

Instructions:

1. In the mixing bowl, dissolve yeast in warm milk. Let it sit for 5 minutes until frothy.
2. Add 2 cups flour, sugar, salt, and eggs. Attach the dough hook and mix on low speed until combined.
3. Gradually add remaining flour, 1/2 cup at a time, until dough forms and pulls away from the sides.
4. Add butter, 1 tablespoon at a time, and knead on medium speed for 10 minutes until dough is smooth and elastic.
5. Place dough in a greased bowl, cover with a damp cloth, and let rise in a warm place for 1 hour or until doubled in size.
6. Punch down dough, shape into a loaf, and place in a greased loaf pan. Cover and let rise for another hour.
7. Preheat oven to 375°F (190°C). Bake for 30-35 minutes until golden brown and hollow sounding when tapped.
8. Cool on a wire rack before slicing.

Focaccia

Servings: 1 loaf (12 slices)

Cooking Time: 3 hours (including rising time)

Ingredients:

- 2 1/4 tsp active dry yeast
- 1 1/2 cups warm water (110°F/45°C)
- 3 1/2 cups bread flour
- 1/4 cup olive oil, plus extra for topping
- 1 tbsp salt
- 1 tbsp fresh rosemary, chopped
- 1 tbsp sea salt

Instructions:

1. In the mixing bowl, dissolve yeast in warm water. Let it sit for 5 minutes until frothy.
2. Add 2 cups flour, olive oil, and salt. Attach the dough hook and mix on low speed until combined.
3. Gradually add remaining flour, 1/2 cup at a time, until dough forms and pulls away from the sides.
4. Knead on medium speed for 8 minutes until dough is smooth and elastic.
5. Place dough in a greased bowl, cover with a damp cloth, and let rise in a warm place for 1 hour or until doubled in size.
6. Punch down dough, shape into a flat oval, and place on a greased baking sheet. Cover and let rise for another hour.
7. Preheat oven to 400°F (200°C). Make indentations in the dough with your fingers, drizzle with olive oil, and sprinkle with rosemary and sea salt.
8. Bake for 20-25 minutes until golden brown.

9. Cool on a wire rack before slicing.

Rye Bread

Servings: 1 loaf (12 slices)

Cooking Time: 3 hours (including rising time)

Ingredients:

- 2 1/4 tsp active dry yeast
- 1 1/4 cups warm water (110°F/45°C)
- 2 cups rye flour
- 2 cups bread flour
- 1 tbsp caraway seeds
- 1 tbsp molasses
- 1 tsp salt

Instructions:

1. In the mixing bowl, dissolve yeast in warm water. Let it sit for 5 minutes until frothy.
2. Add rye flour, 1 cup bread flour, caraway seeds, molasses, and salt. Attach the dough hook and mix on low speed until combined.
3. Gradually add remaining bread flour, 1/2 cup at a time, until dough forms and pulls away from the sides.
4. Knead on medium speed for 8 minutes until dough is smooth and elastic.
5. Place dough in a greased bowl, cover with a damp cloth, and let rise in a warm place for 1 hour or until doubled in size.
6. Punch down dough, shape into a loaf, and place in a greased loaf pan. Cover and let rise for another 30 minutes.
7. Preheat oven to 375°F (190°C). Bake for 30-35 minutes until golden brown and hollow sounding when tapped.
8. Cool on a wire rack before slicing.

Ciabatta

Servings: 2 loaves (16 slices)

Cooking Time: 4 hours (including rising time)

Ingredients:

- 2 1/4 tsp active dry yeast
- 1 1/2 cups warm water (110°F/45°C)
- 4 cups bread flour
- 1 tsp salt
- 2 tbsp olive oil

Instructions:

1. In the mixing bowl, dissolve yeast in warm water. Let it sit for 5 minutes until frothy.
2. Add 2 cups flour and salt. Attach the dough hook and mix on low speed until combined.
3. Gradually add remaining flour, 1/2 cup at a time, until dough forms and pulls away from the sides.
4. Knead on medium speed for 8 minutes until dough is smooth and elastic.
5. Place dough in a greased bowl, cover with a damp cloth, and let rise in a warm place for 1 hour or until doubled in size.
6. Punch down dough, divide in half, and shape into two loaves. Place on a greased baking sheet, cover, and let rise for another hour.
7. Preheat oven to 425°F (220°C). Bake for 25-30 minutes until golden brown and hollow sounding when tapped.
8. Cool on a wire rack before slicing.

Pita Bread

Servings: 8 pitas

Cooking Time: 2 hours (including rising time)

Ingredients:

- 2 1/4 tsp active dry yeast
- 1 1/4 cups warm water (110°F/45°C)
- 3 cups bread flour
- 1 tbsp olive oil
- 1 tsp salt

Instructions:

1. In the mixing bowl, dissolve yeast in warm water. Let it sit for 5 minutes until frothy.
2. Add 1 1/2 cups flour, olive oil, and salt. Attach the dough hook and mix on low speed until combined.
3. Gradually add remaining flour, 1/2 cup at a time, until dough forms and pulls away from the sides.
4. Knead on medium speed for 8 minutes until dough is smooth and elastic.
5. Place dough in a greased bowl, cover with a damp cloth, and let rise in a warm place for 1 hour or until doubled in size.
6. Punch down dough, divide into 8 equal pieces, and shape into balls. Roll each ball into a 1/4-inch thick circle.
7. Preheat oven to 475°F (245°C). Place pitas on a greased baking sheet and bake for 10-12 minutes until puffed and lightly browned.
8. Cool on a wire rack before serving.

Bagels

Servings: 8 bagels

Cooking Time: 3 hours (including rising time)

Ingredients:

- 2 1/4 tsp active dry yeast
- 1 1/4 cups warm water (110°F/45°C)
- 1 tbsp sugar
- 3 1/2 cups bread flour
- 1 1/2 tsp salt
- 1 tbsp barley malt syrup (optional)

Instructions:

1. In the mixing bowl, dissolve yeast in warm water with sugar. Let it sit for 5 minutes until frothy.
2. Add 2 cups flour and salt. Attach the dough hook and mix on low speed until combined.
3. Gradually add remaining flour, 1/2 cup at a time, until dough forms and pulls away from the sides.
4. Knead on medium speed for 8 minutes until dough is smooth and elastic.
5. Place dough in a greased bowl, cover with a damp cloth, and let rise in a warm place for 1 hour or until doubled in size.
6. Punch down dough, divide into 8 equal pieces, and shape into balls. Poke a hole through the center of each ball and gently stretch to form a bagel shape.
7. Preheat oven to 425°F (220°C). Bring a large pot of water to a boil and add barley malt syrup. Boil bagels for 1 minute on each side, then transfer to a greased baking sheet.
8. Bake for 20-25 minutes until golden brown.

9. Cool on a wire rack before serving.

Cinnamon Rolls

Servings: 12 rolls

Cooking Time: 3 hours (including rising time)

Ingredients:

- 2 1/4 tsp active dry yeast
- 1 cup warm milk (110°F/45°C)
- 1/2 cup sugar
- 1/3 cup unsalted butter, melted
- 1 tsp salt
- 2 eggs
- 4 cups bread flour

Filling:

- 1/2 cup unsalted butter, softened
- 1 cup brown sugar
- 2 tbsp ground cinnamon

Icing:

- 1 1/2 cups powdered sugar
- 1/4 cup cream cheese, softened
- 1/4 cup unsalted butter, softened
- 1/2 tsp vanilla extract

Instructions:

1. In the mixing bowl, dissolve yeast in warm milk with sugar. Let it sit for 5 minutes until frothy.
2. Add melted butter, salt, eggs, and 2 cups flour. Attach the dough hook and mix on low speed until combined.
3. Gradually add remaining flour, 1/2 cup at a time, until dough forms and pulls away from the sides.
4. Knead on medium speed for 8 minutes until dough is smooth and elastic.
5. Place dough in a greased bowl, cover with a damp cloth, and let rise in a warm place for 1 hour or until doubled in size.
6. Punch down dough, roll out into a rectangle, and spread with softened butter. Sprinkle with brown sugar and cinnamon.
7. Roll up dough tightly, cut into 12 rolls, and place in a greased baking dish. Cover and let rise for another 30 minutes.
8. Preheat oven to 375°F (190°C). Bake for 20-25 minutes until golden brown.
9. Mix icing ingredients and spread over warm rolls before serving.

Challah

Servings: 1 loaf (12 slices)

Cooking Time: 3 hours (including rising time)

Ingredients:

- 2 1/4 tsp active dry yeast
- 1 cup warm water (110°F/45°C)
- 1/4 cup sugar
- 1/4 cup honey
- 4 cups bread flour
- 2 tsp salt
- 2 large eggs
- 1/4 cup vegetable oil

Instructions:

1. In the mixing bowl, dissolve yeast in warm water with sugar. Let it sit for 5 minutes until frothy.
2. Add honey, 2 cups flour, salt, eggs, and vegetable oil. Attach the dough hook and mix on low speed until combined.
3. Gradually add remaining flour, 1/2 cup at a time, until dough forms and pulls away from the sides.
4. Knead on medium speed for 8 minutes until dough is smooth and elastic.
5. Place dough in a greased bowl, cover with a damp cloth, and let rise in a warm place for 1 hour or until doubled in size.
6. Punch down dough, divide into three equal pieces, and braid. Place on a greased baking sheet, cover, and let rise for another 30 minutes.
7. Preheat oven to 375°F (190°C). Brush with beaten egg and bake for 30-35 minutes until golden brown.
8. Cool on a wire rack before slicing.

Naan

Servings: 8 naans

Cooking Time: 2 hours (including rising time)

Ingredients:

- 2 1/4 tsp active dry yeast
- 1/4 cup warm water (110°F/45°C)
- 1 tsp sugar
- 3 1/2 cups bread flour
- 1/2 cup plain yogurt
- 1/4 cup melted butter
- 1 tsp salt
- 1/2 tsp baking powder

Instructions:

1. In the mixing bowl, dissolve yeast in warm water with sugar. Let it sit for 5 minutes until frothy.
2. Add 1 1/2 cups flour, yogurt, melted butter, salt, and baking powder. Attach the dough hook and mix on low speed until combined.
3. Gradually add remaining flour, 1/2 cup at a time, until dough forms and pulls away from the sides.
4. Knead on medium speed for 8 minutes until dough is smooth and elastic.
5. Place dough in a greased bowl, cover with a damp cloth, and let rise in a warm place for 1 hour or until doubled in size.
6. Punch down dough, divide into 8 equal pieces, and roll each into a ball. Roll out each ball into a thin oval.
7. Preheat a skillet over medium-high heat. Cook each naan for 1-2 minutes on each side until puffed and golden brown.
8. Brush with melted butter before serving.

English Muffins

Servings: 12 muffins

Cooking Time: 3 hours (including rising time)

Ingredients:

- 2 1/4 tsp active dry yeast
- 1 1/4 cups warm water (110°F/45°C)
- 1 tbsp sugar
- 3 1/2 cups bread flour
- 1 tsp salt
- 1/4 cup cornmeal (for dusting)

Instructions:

1. In the mixing bowl, dissolve yeast in warm water with sugar. Let it sit for 5 minutes until frothy.

2. Add 2 cups flour and salt. Attach the dough hook and mix on low speed until combined.
3. Gradually add remaining flour, 1/2 cup at a time, until dough forms and pulls away from the sides.
4. Knead on medium speed for 8 minutes until dough is smooth and elastic.
5. Place dough in a greased bowl, cover with a damp cloth, and let rise in a warm place for 1 hour or until doubled in size.
6. Punch down dough, roll out to 1/2-inch thickness, and cut into 3-inch rounds. Dust with cornmeal and place on a greased baking sheet. Cover and let rise for another 30 minutes.
7. Preheat a skillet over medium heat. Cook each muffin for 5-7 minutes on each side until golden brown.
8. Cool on a wire rack before serving.

Pretzels

Servings: 12 pretzels

Cooking Time: 2 hours (including rising time)

Ingredients:

- 2 1/4 tsp active dry yeast
- 1 1/2 cups warm water (110°F/45°C)
- 1 tbsp sugar
- 4 cups bread flour
- 1 tsp salt
- 1/4 cup baking soda (for boiling)
- 1 egg, beaten (for egg wash)
- Coarse salt (for topping)

Instructions:

1. In the mixing bowl, dissolve yeast in warm water with sugar. Let it sit for 5 minutes until frothy.
2. Add 2 cups flour and salt. Attach the dough hook and mix on low speed until combined.
3. Gradually add remaining flour, 1/2 cup at a time, until dough forms and pulls away from the sides.
4. Knead on medium speed for 8 minutes until dough is smooth and elastic.
5. Place dough in a greased bowl, cover with a damp cloth, and let rise in a warm place for 1 hour or until doubled in size.
6. Preheat oven to 450°F (230°C). Punch down dough, divide into 12 equal pieces, and roll each into a rope. Shape into pretzels.
7. Bring a large pot of water to a boil and add baking soda. Boil pretzels for 30 seconds, then transfer to a greased baking sheet.
8. Brush with beaten egg and sprinkle with coarse salt.
9. Bake for 12-15 minutes until golden brown.
10.   Cool on a wire rack before serving.

Chapter 3: Cakes and Cupcakes

Cakes and cupcakes are a delightful way to celebrate any occasion. The KitchenAid Stand Mixer makes it easier to achieve professional-quality results at home. This chapter covers the basics of cake baking, focusing on mixing techniques for light and fluffy cakes and the effective use of the paddle and whisk attachments. Included are delectable cake and cupcake recipes.

Mixing Techniques for Light and Fluffy Cakes

Creating a cake with a light and fluffy texture involves several important steps:

Creaming Butter and Sugar: This is the process of beating butter and sugar together until they become light and fluffy. This step is crucial as it incorporates air into the batter, which helps the cake rise. Use the paddle attachment for creaming. Start at a low speed to combine the ingredients, then increase to medium-high speed for 3-5 minutes until the mixture is pale and fluffy.

Incorporating Eggs: Add eggs one at a time, beating well after each addition. This helps to emulsify the batter and further incorporates air. Use the paddle attachment on medium speed to mix in the eggs.

Alternating Dry and Wet Ingredients: When adding dry ingredients (like flour) and wet ingredients (like milk or buttermilk), do so in alternating batches. This prevents the batter from becoming too dry or too wet, ensuring a smooth, even texture. Begin and end with the dry ingredients, mixing on low speed to avoid overmixing.

Folding in Additions: Gently fold in any additional ingredients, such as chocolate chips, nuts, or fruit, using a spatula. This prevents the batter from deflating, preserving the air bubbles you've worked to incorporate.

Cakes and Cupcakes Recipes

Classic Vanilla Cake

Servings: 12 slices

Cooking Time: 1 hour 30 minutes

Ingredients:

- 2 1/2 cups all-purpose flour
- 2 1/2 tsp baking powder
- 1/2 tsp salt
- 1 cup unsalted butter, softened
- 2 cups granulated sugar
- 4 large eggs
- 1 cup whole milk
- 2 tsp vanilla extract

Instructions:

1. Preheat oven to 350°F (175°C). Grease and flour two 9-inch round cake pans.
2. In a bowl, whisk together flour, baking powder, and salt.
3. In the mixing bowl, beat butter and sugar with the paddle attachment on medium speed until light and fluffy, about 3-4 minutes.
4. Add eggs one at a time, beating well after each addition. Mix in vanilla extract.
5. With the mixer on low speed, add flour mixture in three additions, alternating with milk, beginning and ending with flour. Mix until just combined.
6. Divide batter evenly between prepared pans. Bake for 25-30 minutes, or until a toothpick inserted into the center comes out clean.
7. Cool in pans for 10 minutes, then transfer to a wire rack to cool completely before frosting.

Chocolate Cupcakes

Servings: 12 cupcakes

Cooking Time: 1 hour

Ingredients:

- 1 cup all-purpose flour
- 1/2 cup cocoa powder
- 1 tsp baking powder
- 1/2 tsp baking soda
- 1/4 tsp salt
- 1/2 cup unsalted butter, softened
- 1 cup granulated sugar
- 2 large eggs
- 1 tsp vanilla extract
- 1/2 cup buttermilk

Instructions:

1. Preheat oven to 350°F (175°C). Line a 12-cup muffin tin with cupcake liners.
2. In a bowl, whisk together flour, cocoa powder, baking powder, baking soda, and salt.
3. In the mixing bowl, beat butter and sugar with the paddle attachment on medium speed until light and fluffy, about 3 minutes.
4. Add eggs one at a time, beating well after each addition. Mix in vanilla extract.
5. With the mixer on low speed, add flour mixture in three additions, alternating with buttermilk, beginning and ending with flour. Mix until just combined.
6. Divide batter evenly among cupcake liners. Bake for 18-20 minutes, or until a toothpick inserted into the center comes out clean.
7. Cool in the tin for 5 minutes, then transfer to a wire rack to cool completely before frosting.

Red Velvet Cake

Servings: 12 slices

Cooking Time: 1 hour 45 minutes

Ingredients:

- 2 1/2 cups all-purpose flour
- 2 tbsp cocoa powder
- 1 tsp baking powder
- 1/2 tsp baking soda
- 1/2 tsp salt
- 1/2 cup unsalted butter, softened
- 1 1/2 cups granulated sugar
- 2 large eggs
- 1 cup buttermilk
- 1/4 cup vegetable oil
- 2 tbsp red food coloring
- 1 tsp vanilla extract
- 1 tsp white vinegar

Instructions:

1. Preheat oven to 350°F (175°C). Grease and flour two 9-inch round cake pans.
2. In a bowl, whisk together flour, cocoa powder, baking powder, baking soda, and salt.
3. In the mixing bowl, beat butter and sugar with the paddle attachment on medium speed until light and fluffy, about 3-4 minutes.
4. Add eggs one at a time, beating well after each addition. Mix in oil, food coloring, vanilla extract, and vinegar.
5. With the mixer on low speed, add flour mixture in three additions, alternating with buttermilk, beginning and ending with flour. Mix until just combined.
6. Divide batter evenly between prepared pans. Bake for 25-30 minutes, or until a toothpick inserted into the center comes out clean.
7. Cool in pans for 10 minutes, then transfer to a wire rack to cool completely before frosting.

Lemon Pound Cake

Servings: 10 slices

Cooking Time: 1 hour 30 minutes

Ingredients:

- 1 1/2 cups all-purpose flour
- 1/2 tsp baking powder
- 1/2 tsp salt
- 1 cup unsalted butter, softened
- 1 cup granulated sugar
- 4 large eggs
- 1/4 cup sour cream
- 1 tbsp lemon zest
- 1/4 cup lemon juice
- 1 tsp vanilla extract

Instructions:

1. Preheat oven to 350°F (175°C). Grease and flour a 9x5-inch loaf pan.
2. In a bowl, whisk together flour, baking powder, and salt.
3. In the mixing bowl, beat butter and sugar with the paddle attachment on medium speed until light and fluffy, about 3-4 minutes.
4. Add eggs one at a time, beating well after each addition. Mix in sour cream, lemon zest, lemon juice, and vanilla extract.
5. With the mixer on low speed, add flour mixture and mix until just combined.
6. Pour batter into prepared pan and smooth the top.
7. Bake for 60-70 minutes, or until a toothpick inserted into the center comes out clean.
8. Cool in the pan for 10 minutes, then transfer to a wire rack to cool completely before slicing.

Carrot Cake

Servings: 12 slices

Cooking Time: 1 hour 45 minutes

Ingredients:

- 2 cups all-purpose flour
- 2 tsp baking powder
- 1 tsp baking soda
- 1/2 tsp salt
- 1 1/2 tsp ground cinnamon
- 1/2 tsp ground nutmeg
- 1/4 tsp ground ginger
- 1 cup vegetable oil
- 1 1/2 cups granulated sugar
- 4 large eggs
- 2 cups grated carrots
- 1/2 cup crushed pineapple, drained
- 1/2 cup chopped walnuts (optional)

Instructions:

1. Preheat oven to 350°F (175°C). Grease and flour two 9-inch round cake pans.
2. In a bowl, whisk together flour, baking powder, baking soda, salt, cinnamon, nutmeg, and ginger.
3. In the mixing bowl, beat oil and sugar with the paddle attachment on medium speed until well combined.
4. Add eggs one at a time, beating well after each addition.
5. With the mixer on low speed, add flour mixture and mix until just combined. Stir in grated carrots, pineapple, and walnuts.
6. Divide batter evenly between prepared pans. Bake for 25-30 minutes, or until a toothpick inserted into the center comes out clean.
7. Cool in pans for 10 minutes, then transfer to a wire rack to cool completely before frosting.

Banana Cupcakes

Servings: 12 cupcakes

Cooking Time: 1 hour

Ingredients:

- 1 1/2 cups all-purpose flour
- 1 tsp baking powder
- 1/2 tsp baking soda
- 1/4 tsp salt
- 1/2 cup unsalted butter, softened
- 1 cup granulated sugar
- 2 large eggs
- 1 tsp vanilla extract
- 1 cup mashed ripe bananas (about 2 bananas)
- 1/4 cup buttermilk

Instructions:

1. Preheat oven to 350°F (175°C). Line a 12-cup muffin tin with cupcake liners.
2. In a bowl, whisk together flour, baking powder, baking soda, and salt.
3. In the mixing bowl, beat butter and sugar with the paddle attachment on medium speed until light and fluffy, about 3 minutes.
4. Add eggs one at a time, beating well after each addition. Mix in vanilla extract and mashed bananas.
5. With the mixer on low speed, add flour mixture in three additions, alternating with buttermilk, beginning and ending with flour. Mix until just combined.
6. Divide batter evenly among cupcake liners. Bake for 18-20 minutes, or until a toothpick inserted into the center comes out clean.
7. Cool in the tin for 5 minutes, then transfer to a wire rack to cool completely before frosting.

Coconut Cake

Servings: 12 slices

Cooking Time: 1 hour 45 minutes

Ingredients:

- 2 1/4 cups all-purpose flour
- 2 tsp baking powder
- 1/2 tsp salt
- 1 cup unsalted butter, softened
- 2 cups granulated sugar
- 4 large eggs
- 1 cup coconut milk
- 1 tsp vanilla extract
- 1/2 tsp coconut extract
- 1 cup shredded coconut

Instructions:

1. Preheat oven to 350°F (175°C). Grease and flour two 9-inch round cake pans.
2. In a bowl, whisk together flour, baking powder, and salt.
3. In the mixing bowl, beat butter and sugar with the paddle attachment on medium speed until light and fluffy, about 3-4 minutes.
4. Add eggs one at a time, beating well after each addition. Mix in vanilla extract and coconut extract.
5. With the mixer on low speed, add flour mixture in three additions, alternating with coconut milk, beginning and ending with flour. Mix until just combined. Stir in shredded coconut.
6. Divide batter evenly between prepared pans. Bake for 25-30 minutes, or until a toothpick inserted into the center comes out clean.
7. Cool in pans for 10 minutes, then transfer to a wire rack to cool completely before frosting.

Marble Cake

Servings: 12 slices

Cooking Time: 1 hour 30 minutes

Ingredients:

- 2 1/4 cups all-purpose flour
- 2 1/2 tsp baking powder
- 1/2 tsp salt
- 1 cup unsalted butter, softened
- 1 1/2 cups granulated sugar
- 4 large eggs
- 1 cup whole milk
- 2 tsp vanilla extract
- 1/4 cup cocoa powder

Instructions:

1. Preheat oven to 350°F (175°C). Grease and flour a 9x5-inch loaf pan.
2. In a bowl, whisk together flour, baking powder, and salt.
3. In the mixing bowl, beat butter and sugar with the paddle attachment on medium speed until light and fluffy, about 3-4 minutes.
4. Add eggs one at a time, beating well after each addition. Mix in vanilla extract.
5. With the mixer on low speed, add flour mixture in three additions, alternating with milk, beginning and ending with flour. Mix until just combined.
6. Divide batter into two bowls. Stir cocoa powder into one bowl of batter.
7. Alternate spoonfuls of vanilla and chocolate batter into the prepared pan. Swirl together with a knife for a marbled effect.
8. Bake for 60-70 minutes, or until a toothpick inserted into the center comes out clean.
9. Cool in the pan for 10 minutes, then transfer to a wire rack to cool completely before slicing.

Orange Chiffon Cake

Servings: 12 slices

Cooking Time: 1 hour 45 minutes

Ingredients:

- 2 1/4 cups cake flour
- 1 1/2 cups granulated sugar, divided
- 1 tbsp baking powder
- 1/2 tsp salt
- 1/2 cup vegetable oil
- 7 large eggs, separated
- 3/4 cup orange juice
- 1 tbsp orange zest
- 1/2 tsp cream of tartar

Instructions:

1. Preheat oven to 325°F (165°C). Do not grease the pan.
2. In the mixing bowl, whisk together flour, 1 cup sugar, baking powder, and salt.
3. Make a well in the center and add oil, egg yolks, orange juice, and orange zest. Beat with the paddle attachment on medium speed until smooth.
4. In a separate mixing bowl, whisk egg whites with the whisk attachment on medium speed until foamy. Add cream of tartar and beat until soft peaks form.
5. Gradually add remaining 1/2 cup sugar and beat until stiff peaks form.
6. Gently fold egg whites into batter until well combined.
7. Pour batter into an ungreased tube pan. Bake for 55-60 minutes, or until a toothpick inserted into the center comes out clean.
8. Invert the pan and cool completely before removing the cake.

Chocolate Lava Cakes

Servings: 6 cakes

Cooking Time: 1 hour

Ingredients:

- 1/2 cup unsalted butter
- 8 oz bittersweet chocolate, chopped
- 1 cup powdered sugar
- 2 large eggs
- 2 large egg yolks
- 6 tbsp all-purpose flour
- 1/4 tsp salt
- Vanilla ice cream (for serving)

Instructions:

1. Preheat oven to 425°F (220°C). Grease six 6-ounce ramekins and dust with cocoa powder.
2. In a heatproof bowl, melt butter and chocolate together over simmering water, stirring until smooth. Remove from heat and stir in powdered sugar.
3. In the mixing bowl, beat eggs and egg yolks with the paddle attachment on medium speed until thick and pale, about 3 minutes.
4. Gradually add melted chocolate mixture and beat until combined.
5. With the mixer on low speed, add flour and salt, mixing until just combined.
6. Divide batter evenly among prepared ramekins. Place ramekins on a baking sheet.
7. Bake for 12-14 minutes, or until edges are firm but centers are still soft.
8. Let stand for 1 minute, then run a knife around the edges to loosen. Invert cakes onto plates and serve warm with vanilla ice cream.

Strawberry Shortcake

Servings: 8 shortcakes

Cooking Time: 1 hour

Ingredients:

- 2 cups all-purpose flour
- 1/4 cup granulated sugar
- 1 tbsp baking powder
- 1/2 tsp salt
- 1/2 cup unsalted butter, cold and cubed
- 2/3 cup whole milk
- 1 tsp vanilla extract
- 1 lb strawberries, hulled and sliced
- 1/4 cup granulated sugar (for strawberries)
- 1 cup heavy cream
- 2 tbsp powdered sugar
- 1/2 tsp vanilla extract (for cream)

Instructions:

1. Preheat oven to 425°F (220°C). Line a baking sheet with parchment paper.
2. In a bowl, whisk together flour, sugar, baking powder, and salt.
3. Cut in cold butter with a pastry blender or two forks until mixture resembles coarse crumbs.
4. Stir in milk and vanilla extract until just combined.
5. Drop dough by 1/4 cupfuls onto prepared baking sheet. Bake for 12-15 minutes, or until golden brown.
6. Cool shortcakes on a wire rack.
7. In a bowl, toss sliced strawberries with 1/4 cup sugar. Let stand for 30 minutes.
8. In the mixing bowl, beat heavy cream, powdered sugar, and vanilla extract with the whisk attachment on medium speed until soft peaks form.
9. Split shortcakes in half, spoon strawberries over bottom halves, and top with whipped cream. Replace tops and serve.

Black Forest Cake

Servings: 12 slices

Cooking Time: 2 hours

Ingredients:

- 1 3/4 cups all-purpose flour
- 2 cups granulated sugar
- 3/4 cup unsweetened cocoa powder
- 1 1/2 tsp baking powder
- 1 1/2 tsp baking soda
- 1 tsp salt
- 2 large eggs
- 1 cup whole milk
- 1/2 cup vegetable oil
- 2 tsp vanilla extract
- 1 cup boiling water
- 2 cups heavy cream
- 1/4 cup powdered sugar
- 1/2 tsp vanilla extract (for cream)
- 1 can (21 oz) cherry pie filling
- Chocolate shavings (for garnish)

Instructions:

1. Preheat oven to 350°F (175°C). Grease and flour two 9-inch round cake pans.
2. In the mixing bowl, whisk together flour, sugar, cocoa powder, baking powder, baking soda, and salt.
3. Add eggs, milk, oil, and vanilla extract. Beat with the paddle attachment on medium speed for 2 minutes.
4. Stir in boiling water (batter will be thin).
5. Divide batter evenly between prepared pans. Bake for 30-35 minutes, or until a toothpick inserted into the center comes out clean.
6. Cool in pans for 10 minutes, then transfer to a wire rack to cool completely.
7. In the mixing bowl, beat heavy cream, powdered sugar, and vanilla extract with the whisk attachment on medium speed until stiff peaks form.

8. To assemble, place one cake layer on a serving plate. Spread with half of the cherry pie filling and top with a layer of whipped cream.
9. Place second cake layer on top and spread with remaining cherry pie filling and whipped cream.
10.   Garnish with chocolate shavings. Chill for 1 hour before serving.

Pumpkin Spice Cupcakes

Servings: 12 cupcakes

Cooking Time: 1 hour

Ingredients:

- 1 1/2 cups all-purpose flour
- 1 tsp baking powder
- 1/2 tsp baking soda
- 1/4 tsp salt
- 1 tsp ground cinnamon
- 1/2 tsp ground ginger
- 1/4 tsp ground nutmeg
- 1/4 tsp ground cloves
- 1/2 cup unsalted butter, softened
- 1 cup granulated sugar
- 2 large eggs
- 1 cup canned pumpkin puree
- 1/4 cup buttermilk

Instructions:

1. Preheat oven to 350°F (175°C). Line a 12-cup muffin tin with cupcake liners.
2. In a bowl, whisk together flour, baking powder, baking soda, salt, cinnamon, ginger, nutmeg, and cloves.
3. In the mixing bowl, beat butter and sugar with the paddle attachment on medium speed until light and fluffy, about 3 minutes.
4. Add eggs one at a time, beating well after each addition. Mix in pumpkin puree.
5. With the mixer on low speed, add flour mixture in three additions, alternating

with buttermilk, beginning and ending with flour. Mix until just combined.
6. Divide batter evenly among cupcake liners. Bake for 18-20 minutes, or until a toothpick inserted into the center comes out clean.
7. Cool in the tin for 5 minutes, then transfer to a wire rack to cool completely before frosting.

Pineapple Upside-Down Cake

Servings: 12 slices

Cooking Time: 1 hour 30 minutes

Ingredients:

- 1/4 cup unsalted butter, melted
- 1/2 cup packed brown sugar
- 1 can (20 oz) pineapple slices, drained
- 10 maraschino cherries
- 1 1/2 cups all-purpose flour
- 1 tsp baking powder
- 1/4 tsp baking soda
- 1/4 tsp salt
- 1/2 cup unsalted butter, softened
- 1 cup granulated sugar
- 2 large eggs
- 1 tsp vanilla extract
- 1/2 cup whole milk
- 1/4 cup pineapple juice

Instructions:

1. Preheat oven to 350°F (175°C). Pour melted butter into a 9-inch round cake pan. Sprinkle brown sugar evenly over butter.
2. Arrange pineapple slices over brown sugar. Place a cherry in the center of each pineapple slice.
3. In a bowl, whisk together flour, baking powder, baking soda, and salt.
4. In the mixing bowl, beat butter and sugar with the paddle attachment on medium

speed until light and fluffy, about 3-4 minutes.

5. Add eggs one at a time, beating well after each addition. Mix in vanilla extract.

6. With the mixer on low speed, add flour mixture in three additions, alternating with milk and pineapple juice, beginning and ending with flour. Mix until just combined.

7. Pour batter over pineapple slices, spreading evenly.

8. Bake for 45-50 minutes, or until a toothpick inserted into the center comes out clean.

9. Cool in the pan for 10 minutes, then invert onto a serving plate. Serve warm or at room temperature.

Tiramisu Cupcakes

Servings: 12 cupcakes

Cooking Time: 1 hour 30 minutes

Ingredients:

- 1 1/2 cups all-purpose flour
- 1 1/2 tsp baking powder
- 1/2 tsp salt
- 1/2 cup unsalted butter, softened
- 1 cup granulated sugar
- 2 large eggs
- 1 tsp vanilla extract
- 1/2 cup whole milk
- 1/4 cup brewed espresso, cooled
- 1 tbsp coffee liqueur (optional)
- 1 cup mascarpone cheese
- 1/2 cup heavy cream
- 1/4 cup powdered sugar
- Unsweetened cocoa powder (for dusting)

Instructions:

1. Preheat oven to 350°F (175°C). Line a 12-cup muffin tin with cupcake liners.

2. In a bowl, whisk together flour, baking powder, and salt.

3. In the mixing bowl, beat butter and sugar with the paddle attachment on medium speed until light and fluffy, about 3 minutes.

4. Add eggs one at a time, beating well after each addition. Mix in vanilla extract.

5. With the mixer on low speed, add flour mixture in three additions, alternating with milk, beginning and ending with flour. Mix until just combined.

6. Divide batter evenly among cupcake liners. Bake for 18-20 minutes, or until a toothpick inserted into the center comes out clean.

7. Cool in the tin for 5 minutes, then transfer to a wire rack to cool completely.

8. In a small bowl, combine espresso and coffee liqueur (if using). Brush over tops of cooled cupcakes.

9. In the mixing bowl, beat mascarpone cheese, heavy cream, and powdered sugar with the whisk attachment on medium speed until smooth and thick.

10. Frost cupcakes with mascarpone mixture and dust with cocoa powder before serving.

Chapter 4: Cookies and Bars

Cookie Dough Mixing Techniques

Creating perfect cookies and bars starts with mastering the techniques for mixing dough. The process can vary depending on the type of cookie, but the fundamentals remain consistent. Here are the essential steps:

- **Creaming Butter and Sugar:** Just like in cake making, creaming butter and sugar is a vital step in cookie dough preparation. It helps to incorporate air into the dough, giving cookies a light and tender texture. Use the paddle attachment at medium speed to cream the butter and sugar until the mixture is light and fluffy, which typically takes about 2-3 minutes.
- **Incorporating Eggs and Flavorings:** Add eggs one at a time, beating well after each addition to ensure proper emulsification. This step helps to create a smooth, homogenous dough. At this stage, also add any liquid flavorings like vanilla extract.
- **Combining Dry Ingredients:** Gradually add the dry ingredients (flour, baking soda, salt, etc.) to the wet mixture. Use a low speed to avoid overmixing, which can result in tough cookies. Mix until just combined.
- **Adding Mix-Ins:** Gently fold in any mix-ins, such as chocolate chips, nuts, or dried fruits, using the paddle attachment on the lowest speed or by hand with a spatula to avoid overworking the dough.

Achieving the Perfect Consistency with the Paddle Attachment

The paddle attachment of your KitchenAid Stand Mixer is designed to evenly mix cookie dough without over-beating. Here are some tips to ensure perfect consistency:

- **Room Temperature Ingredients:** Ensure that ingredients like butter and eggs are at room temperature. This helps them to incorporate more easily and evenly into the dough.
- **Mixing Speed:** Start mixing on a low speed to combine ingredients without creating a cloud of flour. Gradually increase to medium speed for creaming butter and sugar. Always return to low speed when adding dry ingredients to prevent overmixing.
- **Scrape Down the Bowl:** Periodically scrape down the sides and bottom of the bowl to ensure all ingredients are fully incorporated. This prevents pockets of unblended ingredients from affecting the final dough consistency.
- **Chilling the Dough:** For many cookie recipes, chilling the dough before baking can improve the texture and prevent spreading. After mixing, cover the dough and refrigerate for the recommended time in the recip

Cookies and Bars Recipes

Classic Chocolate Chip Cookies

Servings: 24 cookies

Cooking Time: 30 minutes

Ingredients:

- 2 1/4 cups all-purpose flour
- 1/2 tsp baking soda
- 1 cup unsalted butter, room temperature
- 1/2 cup granulated sugar
- 1 cup packed light-brown sugar
- 1 tsp salt
- 2 tsp pure vanilla extract
- 2 large eggs
- 2 cups semisweet and/or milk chocolate chips

Instructions:

1. Preheat oven to 350°F (175°C). Line baking sheets with parchment paper.
2. In a medium bowl, whisk together flour and baking soda; set aside.
3. In the mixing bowl, beat butter and sugars with the paddle attachment on medium speed until light and fluffy, about 3 minutes.
4. Add salt, vanilla, and eggs. Beat until well mixed, about 1 minute.
5. With the mixer on low speed, add flour mixture in batches; mix until just combined.
6. Fold in chocolate chips.
7. Drop dough by rounded tablespoons onto prepared baking sheets, spacing 2 inches apart.
8. Bake until cookies are golden around the edges but still soft in the center, 8 to 10 minutes.
9. Remove from oven, and let cool on baking sheets for 2 minutes. Transfer cookies to a wire rack to cool completely.

Oatmeal Raisin Cookies

Servings: 24 cookies

Cooking Time: 35 minutes

Ingredients:

- 1 1/2 cups all-purpose flour
- 1 tsp baking soda
- 1 tsp ground cinnamon
- 1/2 tsp salt
- 1 cup unsalted butter, room temperature
- 1 cup packed light-brown sugar
- 1/2 cup granulated sugar
- 2 large eggs
- 1 tsp vanilla extract
- 3 cups old-fashioned rolled oats
- 1 cup raisins

Instructions:

1. Preheat oven to 350°F (175°C). Line baking sheets with parchment paper.
2. In a medium bowl, whisk together flour, baking soda, cinnamon, and salt; set aside.
3. In the mixing bowl, beat butter and sugars with the paddle attachment on medium speed until creamy, about 3 minutes.
4. Add eggs and vanilla; beat until combined.
5. Gradually add flour mixture; beat until just combined.
6. Stir in oats and raisins.
7. Drop dough by rounded tablespoons onto prepared baking sheets, spacing 2 inches apart.
8. Bake until edges are lightly browned, 10 to 12 minutes.

9. Let cool on baking sheets for 5 minutes, then transfer to a wire rack to cool completely.

Peanut Butter Cookies

Servings: 24 cookies

Cooking Time: 30 minutes

Ingredients:

- 1 1/4 cups all-purpose flour
- 1/2 tsp baking soda
- 1/4 tsp baking powder
- 1/4 tsp salt
- 1/2 cup unsalted butter, room temperature
- 1 cup peanut butter
- 1/2 cup granulated sugar
- 1/2 cup packed light-brown sugar
- 1 large egg
- 1 tsp vanilla extract

Instructions:

1. Preheat oven to 350°F (175°C). Line baking sheets with parchment paper.
2. In a medium bowl, whisk together flour, baking soda, baking powder, and salt; set aside.
3. In the mixing bowl, beat butter and peanut butter with the paddle attachment on medium speed until smooth, about 1 minute.
4. Add sugars; beat until light and fluffy, about 2 minutes.
5. Add egg and vanilla; beat until combined.
6. Gradually add flour mixture; beat until just combined.
7. Roll dough into 1 1/2-inch balls. Place on prepared baking sheets, spacing 2 inches apart. Flatten each ball with the tines of a fork, making a crisscross pattern.

8. Bake until edges are golden, 10 to 12 minutes.
9. Let cool on baking sheets for 5 minutes, then transfer to a wire rack to cool completely.

Snickerdoodle Cookies

Servings: 24 cookies

Cooking Time: 30 minutes

Ingredients:

- 2 3/4 cups all-purpose flour
- 2 tsp cream of tartar
- 1 tsp baking soda
- 1/4 tsp salt
- 1 cup unsalted butter, room temperature
- 1 1/2 cups granulated sugar
- 2 large eggs
- 1 tsp vanilla extract
- 3 tbsp granulated sugar
- 1 tbsp ground cinnamon

Instructions:

1. Preheat oven to 350°F (175°C). Line baking sheets with parchment paper.
2. In a medium bowl, whisk together flour, cream of tartar, baking soda, and salt; set aside.
3. In the mixing bowl, beat butter and 1 1/2 cups sugar with the paddle attachment on medium speed until light and fluffy, about 3 minutes.
4. Add eggs and vanilla; beat until combined.
5. Gradually add flour mixture; beat until just combined.
6. In a small bowl, combine 3 tablespoons sugar and cinnamon.
7. Roll dough into 1 1/2-inch balls. Roll each ball in cinnamon-sugar mixture. Place on

prepared baking sheets, spacing 2 inches apart.
8. Bake until edges are golden, 8 to 10 minutes.
9. Let cool on baking sheets for 5 minutes, then transfer to a wire rack to cool completely.

Double Chocolate Chip Cookies

Servings: 24 cookies

Cooking Time: 30 minutes

Ingredients:

- 1 cup all-purpose flour
- 1/2 cup unsweetened cocoa powder
- 1/2 tsp baking soda
- 1/4 tsp salt
- 1/2 cup unsalted butter, room temperature
- 1/2 cup granulated sugar
- 1/2 cup packed light-brown sugar
- 1 large egg
- 1 tsp vanilla extract
- 1 cup semisweet chocolate chips

Instructions:

1. Preheat oven to 350°F (175°C). Line baking sheets with parchment paper.
2. In a medium bowl, whisk together flour, cocoa powder, baking soda, and salt; set aside.
3. In the mixing bowl, beat butter and sugars with the paddle attachment on medium speed until light and fluffy, about 3 minutes.
4. Add egg and vanilla; beat until combined.
5. Gradually add flour mixture; beat until just combined.
6. Stir in chocolate chips.
7. Drop dough by rounded tablespoons onto prepared baking sheets, spacing 2 inches apart.

8. Bake until cookies are set, 8 to 10 minutes.
9. Let cool on baking sheets for 5 minutes, then transfer to a wire rack to cool completely.

Lemon Bars

Servings: 24 bars

Cooking Time: 1 hour 15 minutes

Ingredients:

- 2 cups all-purpose flour
- 1/2 cup granulated sugar
- 1/4 tsp salt
- 1 cup unsalted butter, cold and cut into small pieces
- 4 large eggs
- 1 1/2 cups granulated sugar
- 1/2 cup all-purpose flour
- 1 tsp grated lemon zest
- 2/3 cup fresh lemon juice
- Confectioners' sugar, for dusting

Instructions:

1. Preheat oven to 350°F (175°C). Line a 9x13-inch baking pan with parchment paper, leaving an overhang on all sides.
2. In the mixing bowl, combine flour, 1/2 cup sugar, and salt. Add cold butter, and mix with the paddle attachment on low speed until mixture resembles coarse crumbs.
3. Press mixture evenly into the bottom of the prepared pan. Bake until lightly golden, about 20 minutes.
4. Meanwhile, in a medium bowl, whisk together eggs, 1 1/2 cups sugar, 1/2 cup flour, lemon zest, and lemon juice until smooth.
5. Pour filling over hot crust. Bake until filling is set, about 25 minutes.

6. Let cool in the pan on a wire rack. Using the overhang, lift the bars from the pan. Dust with confectioners' sugar before cutting into squares.

Brownies

Servings: 24 brownies

Cooking Time: 45 minutes

Ingredients:

- 1/2 cup unsalted butter
- 1 cup granulated sugar
- 2 large eggs
- 1 tsp vanilla extract
- 1/3 cup unsweetened cocoa powder
- 1/2 cup all-purpose flour
- 1/4 tsp salt
- 1/4 tsp baking powder

Instructions:

1. Preheat oven to 350°F (175°C). Grease and flour an 8x8-inch baking pan.
2. In a medium saucepan, melt butter over medium heat. Remove from heat, and stir in sugar, eggs, and vanilla.
3. Beat in cocoa, flour, salt, and baking powder.
4. Spread batter into prepared pan.
5. Bake in preheated oven for 20 to 25 minutes. Do not overcook.
6. Let cool in pan on a wire rack before cutting into squares.

Blondies

Servings: 24 blondies

Cooking Time: 45 minutes

Ingredients:

- 1 cup unsalted butter, melted
- 2 cups packed light-brown sugar

- 2 large eggs
- 2 tsp vanilla extract
- 2 cups all-purpose flour
- 1 tsp baking powder
- 1/4 tsp baking soda
- 1/2 tsp salt
- 1 cup white chocolate chips

Instructions:

1. Preheat oven to 350°F (175°C). Grease and flour a 9x13-inch baking pan.
2. In the mixing bowl, combine melted butter and brown sugar. Beat with the paddle attachment on medium speed until smooth.
3. Add eggs and vanilla; beat until combined.
4. Gradually add flour, baking powder, baking soda, and salt; beat until just combined.
5. Stir in white chocolate chips.
6. Spread batter evenly into prepared pan.
7. Bake in preheated oven for 25 to 30 minutes, or until a toothpick inserted into the center comes out clean.
8. Let cool in pan on a wire rack before cutting into squares.

Raspberry Bars

Servings: 24 bars

Cooking Time: 1 hour 15 minutes

Ingredients:

- 2 cups all-purpose flour
- 1 cup granulated sugar
- 1/4 tsp salt
- 1 cup unsalted butter, cold and cut into small pieces
- 1/2 cup raspberry jam
- 1/2 cup chopped nuts (optional)

Instructions:

1. Preheat oven to 350°F (175°C). Line a 9x13-inch baking pan with parchment paper, leaving an overhang on all sides.
2. In the mixing bowl, combine flour, sugar, and salt. Add cold butter, and mix with the paddle attachment on low speed until mixture resembles coarse crumbs.
3. Press 2/3 of the mixture evenly into the bottom of the prepared pan. Spread raspberry jam over the crust. Sprinkle remaining crumb mixture and nuts (if using) over jam layer.
4. Bake until lightly golden, about 30 to 35 minutes.
5. Let cool in the pan on a wire rack. Using the overhang, lift the bars from the pan before cutting into squares.

Coconut Macaroons

Servings: 24 macaroons

Cooking Time: 45 minutes

Ingredients:

- 14 oz sweetened shredded coconut
- 14 oz sweetened condensed milk
- 1 tsp vanilla extract
- 2 large egg whites
- 1/4 tsp salt

Instructions:

1. Preheat oven to 325°F (165°C). Line baking sheets with parchment paper.
2. In the mixing bowl, combine coconut, condensed milk, and vanilla with the paddle attachment until well mixed.
3. In a separate bowl, beat egg whites and salt until stiff peaks form.
4. Gently fold egg whites into coconut mixture.
5. Drop batter by rounded tablespoons onto prepared baking sheets.

6. Bake until golden brown, about 25 to 30 minutes.
7. Let cool on baking sheets for 5 minutes, then transfer to a wire rack to cool completely.

S'mores Bars

Servings: 24 bars

Cooking Time: 45 minutes

Ingredients:

- 1/2 cup unsalted butter, room temperature
- 1/4 cup packed light-brown sugar
- 1/2 cup granulated sugar
- 1 large egg
- 1 tsp vanilla extract
- 1 1/3 cups all-purpose flour
- 3/4 cup graham cracker crumbs
- 1 tsp baking powder
- 1/4 tsp salt
- 2 king-size milk chocolate bars
- 1 1/2 cups marshmallow fluff

Instructions:

1. Preheat oven to 350°F (175°C). Grease and flour an 8x8-inch baking pan.
2. In the mixing bowl, beat butter and sugars with the paddle attachment on medium speed until light and fluffy, about 3 minutes.
3. Add egg and vanilla; beat until combined.
4. Gradually add flour, graham cracker crumbs, baking powder, and salt; beat until just combined.
5. Press half of the dough into the bottom of the prepared pan. Place chocolate bars over dough.
6. Spread marshmallow fluff over chocolate. Top with remaining dough, pressing gently.

7. Bake until golden brown, 30 to 35 minutes.
8. Let cool in pan on a wire rack before cutting into squares.

White Chocolate Cranberry Cookies

Servings: 24 cookies

Cooking Time: 30 minutes

Ingredients:

- 1 cup unsalted butter, room temperature
- 1 cup packed light-brown sugar
- 1/2 cup granulated sugar
- 2 large eggs
- 1 tsp vanilla extract
- 2 1/2 cups all-purpose flour
- 1 tsp baking soda
- 1/2 tsp salt
- 1 cup white chocolate chips
- 1 cup dried cranberries

Instructions:

1. Preheat oven to 350°F (175°C). Line baking sheets with parchment paper.
2. In the mixing bowl, beat butter and sugars with the paddle attachment on medium speed until light and fluffy, about 3 minutes.
3. Add eggs and vanilla; beat until combined.
4. Gradually add flour, baking soda, and salt; beat until just combined.
5. Stir in white chocolate chips and dried cranberries.
6. Drop dough by rounded tablespoons onto prepared baking sheets, spacing 2 inches apart.

7. Bake until cookies are golden around the edges but still soft in the center, 8 to 10 minutes.
8. Let cool on baking sheets for 5 minutes, then transfer to a wire rack to cool completely.

Salted Caramel Bars

Servings: 24 bars

Cooking Time: 1 hour 15 minutes

Ingredients:

- 2 cups all-purpose flour
- 1/2 cup granulated sugar
- 1/4 tsp salt
- 1 cup unsalted butter, cold and cut into small pieces
- 1 cup caramel sauce
- 1 tsp sea salt

Instructions:

1. Preheat oven to 350°F (175°C). Line a 9x13-inch baking pan with parchment paper, leaving an overhang on all sides.
2. In the mixing bowl, combine flour, sugar, and salt. Add cold butter, and mix with the paddle attachment on low speed until mixture resembles coarse crumbs.
3. Press mixture evenly into the bottom of the prepared pan. Bake until lightly golden, about 20 minutes.
4. Pour caramel sauce over hot crust. Sprinkle with sea salt.
5. Bake until caramel is set, about 15 minutes.
6. Let cool in the pan on a wire rack. Using the overhang, lift the bars from the pan before cutting into squares.

Ginger Molasses Cookies

Servings: 24 cookies

Cooking Time: 30 minutes

Ingredients:

- 2 1/4 cups all-purpose flour
- 2 tsp ground ginger
- 1 tsp baking soda
- 3/4 tsp ground cinnamon
- 1/2 tsp ground cloves
- 1/4 tsp salt
- 3/4 cup unsalted butter, room temperature
- 1 cup granulated sugar, plus more for rolling
- 1 large egg
- 1/4 cup molasses

Instructions:

1. Preheat oven to 350°F (175°C). Line baking sheets with parchment paper.
2. In a medium bowl, whisk together flour, ginger, baking soda, cinnamon, cloves, and salt; set aside.
3. In the mixing bowl, beat butter and 1 cup sugar with the paddle attachment on medium speed until light and fluffy, about 3 minutes.
4. Add egg and molasses; beat until combined.
5. Gradually add flour mixture; beat until just combined.
6. Roll dough into 1-inch balls. Roll each ball in additional sugar. Place on prepared baking sheets, spacing 2 inches apart.
7. Bake until edges are golden, 8 to 10 minutes.
8. Let cool on baking sheets for 5 minutes, then transfer to a wire rack to cool completely.

Raspberry Almond Bars

Servings: 24 bars

Cooking Time: 1 hour 15 minutes

Ingredients:

- 2 cups all-purpose flour
- 1 cup granulated sugar
- 1/4 tsp salt
- 1 cup unsalted butter, cold and cut into small pieces
- 1/2 cup raspberry jam
- 1/2 cup sliced almonds

Instructions:

1. Preheat oven to 350°F (175°C). Line a 9x13-inch baking pan with parchment paper, leaving an overhang on all sides.
2. In the mixing bowl, combine flour, sugar, and salt. Add cold butter, and mix with the paddle attachment on low speed until mixture resembles coarse crumbs.
3. Press 2/3 of the mixture evenly into the bottom of the prepared pan. Spread raspberry jam over the crust. Sprinkle remaining crumb mixture and sliced almonds over jam layer.
4. Bake until lightly golden, about 30 to 35 minutes.
5. Let cool in the pan on a wire rack. Using the overhang, lift the bars from the pan before cutting into squares.

Chapter 5: Pastries and Pies

Pastry Dough Techniques

Creating tender, flaky pastries and pies requires precision and a good understanding of pastry dough techniques. The key to perfect pastry lies in maintaining the right balance of fat, flour, and liquid, and in handling the dough as little as possible to avoid overworking it.

Using the Paddle and Dough Hook for Perfect Pastry Dough

Your KitchenAid Stand Mixer is a valuable tool for making pastry dough, and both the paddle and dough hook attachments can be used effectively.

1. **Paddle Attachment:**
   - Ideal for initial mixing and cutting in fat (butter or shortening) into the flour. This process is crucial for creating a flaky texture.
   - Steps:
     o Combine flour, salt, and any other dry ingredients in the mixer bowl.
     o Add cold, cubed butter or shortening.
     o Use the paddle attachment on low speed to mix until the fat is incorporated and the mixture resembles coarse crumbs.
2. **Dough Hook Attachment:**
   - Useful for bringing the dough together with minimal handling, which helps to avoid overworking.
   - Steps:
     o After cutting in the fat, gradually add the cold liquid (usually water or milk) while mixing on low speed with the dough hook.
     o Mix until the dough just comes together. It should be crumbly but hold together when pressed.

General Tips for Perfect Pastry Dough

- **Keep Ingredients Cold:** Cold butter and cold water help create a flaky texture by preventing the fat from melting into the flour before baking.
- **Minimal Handling:** Overworking the dough develops gluten, which can make the pastry tough. Mix only until the ingredients are combined.
- **Resting the Dough:** Allowing the dough to rest in the refrigerator for at least 30 minutes helps to relax the gluten and firm up the fat, making it easier to roll out and shape.
- **Rolling Out the Dough:** Roll out the dough on a lightly floured surface, turning it frequently to ensure even thickness and to prevent sticking.

Classic Apple Pie

Servings: 8 slices

Cooking Time: 1 hour 30 minutes

Ingredients:

Crust:

- 2 1/2 cups all-purpose flour
- 1 tsp salt
- 1 cup unsalted butter, cold and cut into cubes
- 6-8 tbsp ice water

Filling:

- 6 cups thinly sliced, peeled apples (Granny Smith or Honeycrisp)
- 3/4 cup granulated sugar
- 1/4 cup packed light-brown sugar
- 1 tsp ground cinnamon
- 1/4 tsp ground nutmeg
- 1 tbsp lemon juice
- 2 tbsp unsalted butter, cut into small pieces

Instructions:

1. Preheat oven to 425°F (220°C).
2. In the mixing bowl, combine flour and salt. Add butter, and mix with the paddle attachment until mixture resembles coarse crumbs. Gradually add ice water, 1 tablespoon at a time, until dough comes together.
3. Divide dough in half, shape into discs, wrap in plastic, and refrigerate for at least 1 hour.
4. Roll out one disc of dough on a floured surface to fit a 9-inch pie plate. Transfer dough to pie plate, trim excess, and refrigerate.
5. In a large bowl, mix apples, sugars, cinnamon, nutmeg, and lemon juice.
6. Pour apple mixture into pie crust, dot with butter.
7. Roll out second disc of dough and place over filling. Trim and crimp edges to seal. Cut slits in top crust to vent.
8. Bake for 45-50 minutes, until crust is golden and filling is bubbly. Cool on a wire rack.

Lemon Meringue Pie

Servings: 8 slices

Cooking Time: 1 hour 30 minutes

Ingredients:

Crust:

- 1 1/4 cups all-purpose flour
- 1/2 tsp salt
- 1/2 cup unsalted butter, cold and cut into cubes
- 3-4 tbsp ice water

Filling:

- 1 cup granulated sugar
- 1/2 cup cornstarch
- 1/4 tsp salt
- 1 1/2 cups water
- 4 large egg yolks, beaten
- 2 tsp grated lemon zest
- 1/2 cup fresh lemon juice
- 2 tbsp unsalted butter

Meringue:

- 4 large egg whites
- 1/4 tsp cream of tartar
- 1/2 cup granulated sugar

Instructions:

1. Preheat oven to 350°F (175°C).
2. In the mixing bowl, combine flour and salt. Add butter, and mix with the paddle attachment until mixture resembles coarse crumbs. Gradually add ice water until dough comes together.
3. Roll out dough on a floured surface to fit a 9-inch pie plate. Transfer dough to pie plate, trim excess, and refrigerate for 30 minutes.
4. Blind bake crust by lining with parchment paper and filling with pie weights. Bake for 15 minutes, remove weights, and bake for another 10 minutes. Let cool.
5. For filling, whisk together sugar, cornstarch, and salt in a saucepan. Gradually whisk in water. Cook over medium heat, stirring constantly, until mixture thickens and boils.
6. Stir a small amount of hot mixture into egg yolks, then return all to pan, stirring constantly. Cook for 2 more minutes. Remove from heat and stir in lemon zest, lemon juice, and butter.
7. Pour hot filling into cooled crust.
8. For meringue, beat egg whites and cream of tartar with whisk attachment until soft peaks form. Gradually add sugar, beating until stiff peaks form. Spread meringue over hot filling, sealing edges to crust.
9. Bake for 12-15 minutes, until meringue is golden. Cool on a wire rack, then refrigerate for at least 2 hours before serving.

Blueberry Hand Pies

Servings: 12 hand pies

Cooking Time: 1 hour 30 minutes

Ingredients:

Crust:

- 2 1/2 cups all-purpose flour
- 1 tsp salt
- 1 cup unsalted butter, cold and cut into cubes
- 6-8 tbsp ice water

Filling:

- 2 cups fresh blueberries
- 1/2 cup granulated sugar
- 1 tbsp cornstarch
- 1 tbsp lemon juice
- 1/2 tsp grated lemon zest
- 1/4 tsp ground cinnamon

Glaze:

- 1 cup powdered sugar
- 2 tbsp milk

Instructions:

1. In the mixing bowl, combine flour and salt. Add butter, and mix with the paddle attachment until mixture resembles coarse crumbs. Gradually add ice water until dough comes together.
2. Divide dough in half, shape into discs, wrap in plastic, and refrigerate for at least 1 hour.
3. Preheat oven to 375°F (190°C). Line baking sheets with parchment paper.
4. In a medium bowl, combine blueberries, sugar, cornstarch, lemon juice, lemon zest, and cinnamon.
5. Roll out one disc of dough on a floured surface to 1/8-inch thickness. Cut into 4-inch circles.
6. Place a tablespoon of filling in the center of each circle. Fold dough over filling, pressing edges to seal. Crimp edges with a fork.
7. Arrange hand pies on prepared baking sheets. Cut small slits in the tops to vent.
8. Bake for 20-25 minutes, until golden brown. Let cool on wire racks.

9. For glaze, whisk together powdered sugar and milk. Drizzle over cooled hand pies.

Chocolate Eclairs

Servings: 12 eclairs

Cooking Time: 1 hour 30 minutes

Ingredients:

Pastry:

- 1/2 cup unsalted butter
- 1 cup water
- 1/4 tsp salt
- 1 cup all-purpose flour
- 4 large eggs

Filling:

- 2 cups whole milk
- 1/2 cup granulated sugar
- 1/4 cup cornstarch
- 1/4 tsp salt
- 4 large egg yolks
- 2 tbsp unsalted butter
- 1 tsp vanilla extract

Glaze:

- 1/2 cup heavy cream
- 4 oz semisweet chocolate, finely chopped

Instructions:

1. Preheat oven to 400°F (200°C). Line baking sheets with parchment paper.
2. In a saucepan, bring butter, water, and salt to a boil. Remove from heat and stir in flour until mixture forms a ball.
3. Transfer dough to the mixing bowl. Using the paddle attachment, beat in eggs one at a time until smooth.
4. Spoon or pipe dough onto prepared baking sheets into 4-inch strips.

5. Bake for 25-30 minutes, until golden brown. Cool on wire racks.
6. For filling, heat milk in a saucepan until simmering. In a bowl, whisk together sugar, cornstarch, and salt. Gradually whisk in hot milk. Return mixture to saucepan and cook, whisking constantly, until thickened.
7. Remove from heat, and whisk in egg yolks, butter, and vanilla. Cover and refrigerate until chilled.
8. For glaze, heat cream in a saucepan until steaming. Pour over chocolate and let sit for 5 minutes. Stir until smooth.
9. To assemble, split eclairs and fill with pastry cream. Dip tops in chocolate glaze.

Pumpkin Pie

Servings: 8 slices

Cooking Time: 1 hour 15 minutes

Ingredients:

Crust:

- 1 1/4 cups all-purpose flour
- 1/2 tsp salt
- 1/2 cup unsalted butter, cold and cut into cubes
- 3-4 tbsp ice water

Filling:

- 1 can (15 oz) pumpkin puree
- 1 cup heavy cream
- 3/4 cup packed light-brown sugar
- 2 large eggs
- 1 tsp ground cinnamon
- 1/2 tsp ground ginger
- 1/4 tsp ground cloves
- 1/4 tsp salt

Instructions:

1. Preheat oven to 425°F (220°C).

2. In the mixing bowl, combine flour and salt. Add butter, and mix with the paddle attachment until mixture resembles coarse crumbs. Gradually add ice water until dough comes together.
3. Roll out dough on a floured surface to fit a 9-inch pie plate. Transfer dough to pie plate, trim excess, and refrigerate for 30 minutes.
4. In a large bowl, whisk together pumpkin puree, cream, brown sugar, eggs, spices, and salt.
5. Pour filling into chilled pie crust.
6. Bake for 15 minutes. Reduce temperature to 350°F (175°C) and bake for an additional 35-40 minutes, until filling is set. Cool on a wire rack before serving.

Almond Croissants

Servings: 8 croissants

Cooking Time: 1 hour 30 minutes

Ingredients:

Dough:

- 2 1/4 cups all-purpose flour
- 1/4 cup granulated sugar
- 1/2 tsp salt
- 1 tbsp active dry yeast
- 1 cup milk, warm
- 1/2 cup unsalted butter, softened
- 1 large egg

Filling:

- 1/2 cup almond paste
- 1/4 cup granulated sugar
- 1/4 cup unsalted butter, softened
- 1/4 tsp almond extract

Topping:

- 1/2 cup sliced almonds

- Powdered sugar for dusting

Instructions:

1. In the mixing bowl, combine flour, sugar, salt, and yeast. Add milk, butter, and egg. Mix with the dough hook attachment until smooth and elastic. Let rise in a warm place for 1 hour, or until doubled in size.
2. Punch down dough, roll out into a rectangle. Cut into 8 triangles.
3. For filling, combine almond paste, sugar, butter, and almond extract until smooth. Spread a small amount on each triangle.
4. Roll up triangles from the wide end to the point. Place on baking sheets lined with parchment paper.
5. Brush with egg wash and sprinkle with sliced almonds.
6. Bake at 375°F (190°C) for 20-25 minutes, until golden brown. Dust with powdered sugar before serving.

Quiche Lorraine

Servings: 8 slices

Cooking Time: 1 hour 15 minutes

Ingredients:

Crust:

- 1 1/4 cups all-purpose flour
- 1/2 tsp salt
- 1/2 cup unsalted butter, cold and cut into cubes
- 3-4 tbsp ice water

Filling:

- 8 oz bacon, cooked and crumbled
- 1 cup shredded Gruyère cheese
- 4 large eggs
- 1 1/2 cups heavy cream
- 1/2 cup milk

- 1/4 tsp salt
- 1/4 tsp ground black pepper

Instructions:

1. Preheat oven to 375°F (190°C).
2. In the mixing bowl, combine flour and salt. Add butter, and mix with the paddle attachment until mixture resembles coarse crumbs. Gradually add ice water until dough comes together.
3. Roll out dough on a floured surface to fit a 9-inch pie plate. Transfer dough to pie plate, trim excess, and refrigerate for 30 minutes.
4. Bake crust for 15 minutes. Remove from oven and sprinkle with bacon and cheese.
5. In a bowl, whisk together eggs, cream, milk, salt, and pepper. Pour over bacon and cheese.
6. Bake for 35-40 minutes, until filling is set and crust is golden. Cool for 10 minutes before slicing.

Strawberry Rhubarb Pie

Servings: 8 slices

Cooking Time: 1 hour 30 minutes

Ingredients:

Crust:

- 2 1/2 cups all-purpose flour
- 1 tsp salt
- 1 cup unsalted butter, cold and cut into cubes
- 6-8 tbsp ice water

Filling:

- 2 cups sliced strawberries
- 2 cups chopped rhubarb
- 1 1/2 cups granulated sugar
- 1/4 cup cornstarch

- 1/4 tsp salt
- 1 tbsp lemon juice

Instructions:

1. Preheat oven to 425°F (220°C).
2. In the mixing bowl, combine flour and salt. Add butter, and mix with the paddle attachment until mixture resembles coarse crumbs. Gradually add ice water until dough comes together.
3. Roll out half of the dough on a floured surface to fit a 9-inch pie plate. Transfer dough to pie plate, trim excess, and refrigerate for 30 minutes.
4. In a large bowl, combine strawberries, rhubarb, sugar, cornstarch, salt, and lemon juice. Mix well and let sit for 10 minutes.
5. Pour filling into the chilled pie crust.
6. Roll out remaining dough and place over filling. Trim and crimp edges to seal. Cut slits in top crust to vent.
7. Bake for 45-50 minutes, until crust is golden and filling is bubbly. Cool on a wire rack before serving.

Peach Galette

Servings: 8 slices

Cooking Time: 1 hour

Ingredients:

Crust:

- 1 1/2 cups all-purpose flour
- 1/4 cup granulated sugar
- 1/4 tsp salt
- 1/2 cup unsalted butter, cold and cut into cubes
- 4-5 tbsp ice water

Filling:

- 4 cups sliced fresh peaches

- 1/2 cup granulated sugar
- 2 tbsp all-purpose flour
- 1/4 tsp ground cinnamon
- 1 tbsp lemon juice

Topping:

- 1 large egg, beaten
- 1 tbsp coarse sugar

Instructions:

- Preheat oven to 375°F (190°C). Line a baking sheet with parchment paper.
- In the mixing bowl, combine flour, sugar, and salt. Add butter, and mix with the paddle attachment until mixture resembles coarse crumbs. Gradually add ice water until dough comes together.
- Roll out dough on a floured surface into a 12-inch circle. Transfer to the prepared baking sheet.
- In a large bowl, combine peaches, sugar, flour, cinnamon, and lemon juice. Place peach mixture in the center of the dough, leaving a 2-inch border.
- Fold edges of dough over filling, pleating as necessary. Brush dough with beaten egg and sprinkle with coarse sugar.
- Bake for 35-40 minutes, until crust is golden and filling is bubbly. Cool on a wire rack before serving.

Pecan Pie

Servings: 8 slices

Cooking Time: 1 hour 15 minutes

Ingredients:

Crust:

- 1 1/4 cups all-purpose flour
- 1/2 tsp salt
- 1/2 cup unsalted butter, cold and cut into cubes

- 3-4 tbsp ice water

Filling:

- 1 cup light corn syrup
- 1 cup granulated sugar
- 1/4 cup unsalted butter, melted
- 3 large eggs
- 1 1/2 cups pecan halves
- 1 tsp vanilla extract

Instructions:

1. Preheat oven to 350°F (175°C).
2. In the mixing bowl, combine flour and salt. Add butter, and mix with the paddle attachment until mixture resembles coarse crumbs. Gradually add ice water until dough comes together.
3. Roll out dough on a floured surface to fit a 9-inch pie plate. Transfer dough to pie plate, trim excess, and refrigerate for 30 minutes.
4. In a large bowl, whisk together corn syrup, sugar, melted butter, eggs, and vanilla.
5. Arrange pecans in the pie crust and pour filling over them.
6. Bake for 50-60 minutes, until filling is set and crust is golden. Cool on a wire rack before serving.

Tarts aux Pommes (French Apple Tart)

Servings: 8 slices

Cooking Time: 1 hour 15 minutes

Ingredients:

Crust:

- 1 1/2 cups all-purpose flour
- 1/4 cup granulated sugar
- 1/4 tsp salt

- 1/2 cup unsalted butter, cold and cut into cubes
- 1 large egg yolk

Filling:

- 4 medium apples (such as Granny Smith or Honeycrisp)
- 1/4 cup granulated sugar
- 1 tbsp lemon juice
- 1/2 tsp ground cinnamon
- 2 tbsp apricot jam

Instructions:

1. Preheat oven to 375°F (190°C). Grease and flour a tart pan.
2. In the mixing bowl, combine flour, sugar, and salt. Add butter, and mix with the paddle attachment until mixture resembles coarse crumbs. Add egg yolk and mix until dough comes together.
3. Press dough evenly into the bottom and sides of the tart pan. Refrigerate for 30 minutes.
4. Bake crust for 15 minutes, then let cool.
5. Peel, core, and thinly slice apples. Arrange slices in a circular pattern over the pre-baked crust.
6. Sprinkle with sugar and cinnamon. Bake for 30-35 minutes, until apples are tender and crust is golden.
7. Brush tart with apricot jam for a glossy finish.

Chocolate Cream Pie

Servings: 8 slices

Cooking Time: 1 hour 30 minutes

Ingredients:

Crust:

- 1 1/2 cups graham cracker crumbs
- 1/4 cup granulated sugar
- 1/4 cup unsalted butter, melted

Filling:

- 1 cup whole milk
- 1 cup heavy cream
- 1/2 cup granulated sugar
- 1/4 cup unsweetened cocoa powder
- 3 tbsp cornstarch
- 1/4 tsp salt
- 4 large egg yolks
- 1 tsp vanilla extract
- 4 oz semisweet chocolate, chopped

Topping:

- 1 cup heavy cream
- 2 tbsp granulated sugar
- Chocolate shavings or cocoa powder, for garnish

Instructions:

1. Preheat oven to 350°F (175°C).
2. In a medium bowl, combine graham cracker crumbs, sugar, and melted butter. Press mixture into the bottom and sides of a 9-inch pie plate.
3. Bake for 10 minutes. Let cool.
4. For filling, in a saucepan, whisk together milk, cream, sugar, cocoa powder, cornstarch, and salt. Cook over medium heat, whisking constantly, until mixture thickens and comes to a boil.
5. Whisk a small amount of hot mixture into egg yolks, then return all to the pan. Cook, whisking constantly, for 2 more minutes. Remove from heat and stir in vanilla and chocolate until smooth.
6. Pour filling into cooled crust. Refrigerate for at least 2 hours, until set.
7. For topping, whip cream with sugar until stiff peaks form. Spread over chilled pie and garnish with chocolate shavings or cocoa powder.

Pear Almond Tart

Servings: 8 slices

Cooking Time: 1 hour 15 minutes

Ingredients:

Crust:

- 1 1/2 cups all-purpose flour
- 1/4 cup granulated sugar
- 1/4 tsp salt
- 1/2 cup unsalted butter, cold and cut into cubes
- 1 large egg yolk

Filling:

- 1/2 cup almond paste
- 1/4 cup granulated sugar
- 1/4 cup unsalted butter, softened
- 1 large egg
- 2 tbsp all-purpose flour
- 2 ripe pears, peeled, cored, and thinly sliced

Topping:

- 1/4 cup sliced almonds
- Powdered sugar for dusting

Instructions:

1. Preheat oven to 375°F (190°C). Grease and flour a tart pan.
2. In the mixing bowl, combine flour, sugar, and salt. Add butter, and mix with the paddle attachment until mixture resembles coarse crumbs. Add egg yolk and mix until dough comes together.
3. Press dough evenly into the bottom and sides of the tart pan. Refrigerate for 30 minutes.
4. Bake crust for 15 minutes, then let cool.
5. For filling, in the mixing bowl, combine almond paste, sugar, butter, egg, and flour with the paddle attachment until smooth. Spread filling over the pre-baked crust.
6. Arrange pear slices in an overlapping pattern over the almond filling. Sprinkle with sliced almonds.
7. Bake for 35-40 minutes, until filling is set and pears are tender. Dust with powdered sugar before serving.

Chocolate Mint Tart

Servings: 8 slices

Cooking Time: 1 hour 30 minutes

Ingredients:

Crust:

- 1 1/2 cups chocolate cookie crumbs
- 1/4 cup granulated sugar
- 1/4 cup unsalted butter, melted

Filling:

- 1 cup heavy cream
- 1 cup semisweet chocolate chips
- 1/4 cup peppermint schnapps or extract
- 2 tbsp granulated sugar

Topping:

- Whipped cream
- Crushed chocolate mint candies

Instructions:

1. Preheat oven to 350°F (175°C).
2. In a medium bowl, combine chocolate cookie crumbs, sugar, and melted butter. Press mixture into the bottom and sides of a 9-inch tart pan.
3. Bake for 10 minutes. Let cool.
4. In a saucepan, heat cream until steaming. Pour over chocolate chips and let sit for 5 minutes. Stir until smooth.

Add peppermint schnapps or extract and sugar, mixing well.

5. Pour filling into cooled crust. Refrigerate for at least 2 hours, until set.
6. Top with whipped cream and crushed chocolate mint candies before serving.

Raspberry Almond Tart

Servings: 8 slices

Cooking Time: 1 hour 15 minutes

Ingredients:

Crust:

- 1 1/2 cups all-purpose flour
- 1/4 cup granulated sugar
- 1/4 tsp salt
- 1/2 cup unsalted butter, cold and cut into cubes
- 1 large egg yolk

Filling:

- 1/2 cup almond paste
- 1/4 cup granulated sugar
- 1/4 cup unsalted butter, softened
- 1 large egg
- 2 tbsp all-purpose flour
- 1/2 cup raspberry preserves

Topping:

- 1/4 cup sliced almonds
- Powdered sugar for dusting

Instructions:

1. Preheat oven to 375°F (190°C). Grease and flour a tart pan.
2. In the mixing bowl, combine flour, sugar, and salt. Add butter, and mix with the paddle attachment until mixture resembles coarse crumbs. Add egg yolk and mix until dough comes together.
3. Press dough evenly into the bottom and sides of the tart pan. Refrigerate for 30 minutes.
4. Bake crust for 15 minutes, then let cool.
5. For filling, in the mixing bowl, combine almond paste, sugar, butter, egg, and flour with the paddle attachment until smooth. Spread filling over the pre-baked crust.
6. Spoon raspberry preserves over filling and swirl gently.
7. Sprinkle with sliced almonds.
8. Bake for 35-40 minutes, until filling is set and almonds are golden. Dust with powdered sugar before serving.

Chapter 6: Savory Dishes

Harness the full potential of your KitchenAid Stand Mixer to create hearty and satisfying main courses. From mixing and kneading to shredding and blending, this chapter provides recipes that demonstrate how your mixer can simplify and enhance your savory cooking.

Your KitchenAid Stand Mixer isn't just for baking sweets; it's a powerful tool for preparing savory dishes as well. This section explores how to use your stand mixer for mixing and shredding techniques to streamline the preparation of main courses.

Shredding Techniques for Main Courses

1. **Shredding Cooked Chicken or Pork:**
   Purpose: Prepare shredded chicken or pork for tacos, sandwiches, or salads.
   Technique: Use the paddle attachment on a low speed to shred cooked, cooled chicken or pork. Ensure the meat is cool before shredding to avoid drying it out.
2. **Pulled Pork:**
   Ingredients: Cooked pork shoulder.
   Procedure: After cooking and cooling the pork, use the paddle attachment to shred the meat in the mixing bowl. Add barbecue sauce or other seasonings as desired.
3. **Cheese Shredding:**
   Purpose: Shred cheese for casseroles, toppings, or stuffing.
   Technique: Use the shredding attachment to grate cheese directly into the mixing bowl. This method is faster than shredding by hand and ensures consistency.

Main Course Recipes

Classic Meatloaf

Servings: 8

Cooking Time: 1 hour 15 minutes

Ingredients:

- 1 lb ground beef
- 1/2 lb ground pork
- 1 cup breadcrumbs
- 1/2 cup milk
- 1/2 cup ketchup
- 1/4 cup finely chopped onion
- 1 large egg
- 1 tbsp Worcestershire sauce
- 1 tsp dried thyme
- 1 tsp salt
- 1/2 tsp black pepper

Instructions:

1. Preheat oven to 375°F (190°C).
2. In the mixing bowl, combine ground beef, ground pork, breadcrumbs, milk, ketchup, onion, egg, Worcestershire sauce, thyme, salt, and pepper. Mix with the paddle attachment until well combined.
3. Shape mixture into a loaf and place in a baking dish.
4. Bake for 1 hour, until cooked through and internal temperature reaches 160°F (70°C). Let rest for 10 minutes before slicing.

Chicken Parmesan

Servings: 4

Cooking Time: 45 minutes

Ingredients:

- 4 boneless, skinless chicken breasts
- 1 cup breadcrumbs
- 1/2 cup grated Parmesan cheese
- 1/2 cup all-purpose flour
- 2 large eggs
- 2 cups marinara sauce
- 1 cup shredded mozzarella cheese
- 1/4 cup chopped fresh basil

Instructions:

1. Preheat oven to 375°F (190°C).
2. In a shallow dish, combine breadcrumbs and Parmesan cheese. In another dish, place flour. In a third dish, beat eggs.
3. Dredge chicken breasts in flour, then dip in eggs, and coat with breadcrumb mixture. Place in a baking dish.
4. Bake for 20 minutes. Remove from oven, top with marinara sauce and mozzarella cheese.
5. Return to oven and bake for an additional 15 minutes, until cheese is melted and bubbly. Garnish with fresh basil.

Classic Beef Stroganoff

Servings: 4

Cooking Time: 1 hour

Ingredients:

- 1 lb beef sirloin, cut into thin strips
- 1 tbsp olive oil
- 1 cup sliced mushrooms
- 1 small onion, chopped
- 2 cloves garlic, minced
- 1 cup beef broth
- 1 cup sour cream
- 2 tbsp flour
- 1 tbsp Dijon mustard
- 1 tbsp Worcestershire sauce

- Salt and pepper to taste
- Fresh parsley for garnish

Instructions:

1. Heat olive oil in a large skillet over medium heat. Add beef strips and cook until browned. Remove and set aside.
2. In the same skillet, add mushrooms, onion, and garlic. Cook until mushrooms are tender.
3. Sprinkle flour over vegetables and stir to combine. Gradually add beef broth, stirring constantly. Bring to a simmer.
4. Stir in sour cream, Dijon mustard, and Worcestershire sauce. Return beef to skillet and cook until heated through. Season with salt and pepper.
5. Garnish with fresh parsley before serving.

Creamy Chicken and Spinach Pasta

Servings: 4

Cooking Time: 30 minutes

Ingredients:

- 2 cups cooked pasta
- 1 lb chicken breast, diced
- 1 tbsp olive oil
- 1 cup heavy cream
- 1/2 cup grated Parmesan cheese
- 2 cups fresh spinach
- 1/2 cup sun-dried tomatoes, chopped
- 2 cloves garlic, minced
- Salt and pepper to taste

Instructions:

1. Heat olive oil in a large skillet over medium heat. Add chicken and cook until browned and cooked through.

2. Add garlic and cook for 1 minute. Stir in sun-dried tomatoes and spinach, cooking until spinach is wilted.
3. Pour in heavy cream and bring to a simmer. Stir in Parmesan cheese until melted and sauce is creamy.
4. Add cooked pasta and toss to coat. Season with salt and pepper.

Spicy Sausage and Pepper Skillet

Servings: 4

Cooking Time: 30 minutes

Ingredients:

- 1 lb Italian sausage, sliced
- 2 tbsp olive oil
- 1 large bell pepper, sliced
- 1 large onion, sliced
- 2 cloves garlic, minced
- 1 can (14.5 oz) diced tomatoes
- 1/2 cup chicken broth
- 1 tsp red pepper flakes
- 1 tsp dried oregano
- Salt and pepper to taste

Instructions:

1. Heat olive oil in a large skillet over medium heat. Add sausage and cook until browned. Remove and set aside.
2. In the same skillet, add bell pepper, onion, and garlic. Cook until vegetables are tender.
3. Stir in diced tomatoes, chicken broth, red pepper flakes, oregano, salt, and pepper. Bring to a simmer.
4. Return sausage to the skillet and cook until heated through. Serve hot.

Chicken Enchiladas

Servings: 6

Cooking Time: 1 hour

Ingredients:

- 2 cups shredded cooked chicken
- 1 can (10 oz) enchilada sauce
- 1 cup shredded cheddar cheese
- 1/2 cup sour cream
- 1/2 cup chopped green onions
- 8-10 flour tortillas
- 1 cup chopped cilantro

Instructions:

1. Preheat oven to 375°F (190°C).
2. In a mixing bowl, combine shredded chicken, 1/2 cup enchilada sauce, 1/2 cup cheese, and green onions.
3. Spoon mixture into tortillas, roll up, and place seam side down in a baking dish.
4. Pour remaining enchilada sauce over the top and sprinkle with remaining cheese.
5. Bake for 25-30 minutes, until cheese is melted and bubbly. Garnish with chopped cilantro.

Savory Beef and Vegetable Pie

Servings: 6

Cooking Time: 1 hour 30 minutes

Ingredients:

Filling:

- 1 lb beef stew meat
- 2 tbsp olive oil
- 1 onion, chopped
- 2 carrots, diced
- 2 potatoes, diced
- 1 cup frozen peas
- 2 cups beef broth

- 1 tbsp tomato paste
- 1 tsp dried thyme
- 1 tsp dried rosemary
- Salt and pepper to taste

Pie Crust:

- 2 1/2 cups all-purpose flour
- 1/2 tsp salt
- 1 cup unsalted butter, cold and cut into cubes
- 6-8 tbsp ice water

Instructions:

1. Preheat oven to 375°F (190°C).
2. In a large skillet, heat olive oil and brown beef on all sides. Remove and set aside.
3. In the same skillet, add onion, carrots, and potatoes. Cook until vegetables are tender.
4. Stir in beef broth, tomato paste, thyme, rosemary, salt, and pepper. Return beef to skillet and simmer for 30 minutes.
5. For crust, combine flour and salt in the mixing bowl. Add butter and mix with the paddle attachment until mixture resembles coarse crumbs. Gradually add ice water until dough comes together.
6. Roll out dough and fit into a pie dish. Pour beef mixture into crust.
7. Roll out remaining dough and place over filling. Trim and crimp edges to seal.
8. Bake for 40-45 minutes, until crust is golden. Let cool before serving.

Turkey Meatballs in Tomato Sauce

Servings: 4

Cooking Time: 45 minutes

Ingredients:

Meatballs:

- 1 lb ground turkey
- 1/2 cup breadcrumbs
- 1/4 cup grated Parmesan cheese
- 1 large egg
- 2 cloves garlic, minced
- 1/4 cup chopped parsley
- 1/2 tsp dried oregano
- Salt and pepper to taste

Sauce:

- 2 cups marinara sauce
- 1/2 cup chopped basil

Instructions:

1. Preheat oven to 375°F (190°C).
2. In the mixing bowl, combine ground turkey, breadcrumbs, Parmesan cheese, egg, garlic, parsley, oregano, salt, and pepper. Mix with the paddle attachment until well combined.
3. Form mixture into meatballs and place on a baking sheet.
4. Bake for 25 minutes, until cooked through.
5. Heat marinara sauce in a large skillet. Add cooked meatballs and simmer for 10 minutes. Garnish with chopped basil.

Beef and Broccoli Stir-Fry

Servings: 4

Cooking Time: 30 minutes

Ingredients:

- 1 lb beef sirloin, thinly sliced
- 2 tbsp vegetable oil
- 2 cups broccoli florets
- 1 bell pepper, sliced
- 1/2 cup soy sauce
- 1/4 cup oyster sauce
- 2 tbsp cornstarch
- 1/4 cup water

- 2 cloves garlic, minced
- 1 tsp ginger, minced
- Cooked rice for serving

Instructions:

1. Heat vegetable oil in a large skillet or wok over high heat. Add beef and cook until browned. Remove and set aside.
2. In the same skillet, add broccoli and bell pepper. Stir-fry for 5 minutes.
3. In a bowl, combine soy sauce, oyster sauce, cornstarch, and water. Pour over vegetables and cook until sauce thickens.
4. Stir in beef and cook for 2 more minutes. Serve over cooked rice.

Spinach and Ricotta Stuffed Shells

Servings: 6

Cooking Time: 1 hour

Ingredients:

- 12 large pasta shells
- 1 cup ricotta cheese
- 1 cup shredded mozzarella cheese
- 1/2 cup grated Parmesan cheese
- 2 cups fresh spinach, chopped
- 1 large egg
- 2 cups marinara sauce
- 1/4 cup chopped fresh basil

Instructions:

1. Preheat oven to 375°F (190°C).
2. Cook pasta shells according to package instructions. Drain and set aside.
3. In a mixing bowl, combine ricotta, mozzarella, Parmesan, spinach, and egg. Mix with the paddle attachment until well blended.

4. Stuff each shell with cheese mixture and place in a baking dish. Pour marinara sauce over shells.
5. Bake for 25-30 minutes, until cheese is melted and bubbly. Garnish with fresh basil.

Shrimp and Grits

Servings: 4

Cooking Time: 30 minutes

Ingredients:

Grits:

- 1 cup quick-cooking grits
- 4 cups water
- 1/2 cup milk
- 1/2 cup shredded cheddar cheese
- 2 tbsp butter

Shrimp:

- 1 lb large shrimp, peeled and deveined
- 2 tbsp olive oil
- 2 cloves garlic, minced
- 1/2 tsp paprika
- 1/4 tsp cayenne pepper
- Salt and pepper to taste

Instructions:

1. In a saucepan, bring water to a boil. Stir in grits, reduce heat, and simmer for 5 minutes, stirring occasionally. Stir in milk, cheddar cheese, and butter until creamy.
2. Heat olive oil in a skillet over medium heat. Add garlic and cook for 1 minute.
3. Add shrimp, paprika, cayenne pepper, salt, and pepper. Cook until shrimp are pink and cooked through.
4. Serve shrimp over grits.

BBQ Pulled Pork

Servings: 6

Cooking Time: 8 hours (slow cooker)

Ingredients:

- 3 lb pork shoulder
- 1 cup BBQ sauce
- 1/2 cup chicken broth
- 1/4 cup apple cider vinegar
- 2 tbsp brown sugar
- 1 tbsp smoked paprika
- 1 tbsp onion powder
- 1 tbsp garlic powder
- 1/2 tsp salt
- 1/2 tsp black pepper

Instructions:

1. Place pork shoulder in the slow cooker.
2. In a bowl, mix BBQ sauce, chicken broth, apple cider vinegar, brown sugar, paprika, onion powder, garlic powder, salt, and pepper. Pour over pork.
3. Cook on low for 8 hours, until pork is tender and easily shreds.
4. Shred pork with the stand mixer's paddle attachment for convenience. Serve with additional BBQ sauce on buns.

Stuffed Bell Peppers

Servings: 4

Cooking Time: 1 hour

Ingredients:

- 4 large bell peppers
- 1 lb ground beef
- 1 cup cooked rice
- 1 cup marinara sauce
- 1/2 cup chopped onion
- 1/2 cup shredded cheddar cheese
- 1 tsp dried oregano

- Salt and pepper to taste

Instructions:

1. Preheat oven to 375°F (190°C).
2. Cut tops off bell peppers and remove seeds. Set aside.
3. In a skillet, cook ground beef and onion until browned. Drain excess fat.
4. In the mixing bowl, combine beef mixture, cooked rice, marinara sauce, cheddar cheese, oregano, salt, and pepper.
5. Stuff mixture into bell peppers and place in a baking dish.
6. Bake for 30-35 minutes, until peppers are tender.

Lentil and Vegetable Stew

Servings: 6

Cooking Time: 1 hour 15 minutes

Ingredients:

- 1 cup dried lentils
- 1 tbsp olive oil
- 1 onion, chopped
- 2 carrots, diced
- 2 celery stalks, diced
- 2 cloves garlic, minced
- 1 can (14.5 oz) diced tomatoes
- 4 cups vegetable broth
- 1 tsp dried thyme
- 1 tsp dried rosemary
- 1 cup frozen peas
- Salt and pepper to taste

Instructions:

1. In a large pot, heat olive oil over medium heat. Add onion, carrots, celery, and garlic. Cook until vegetables are tender.
2. Stir in lentils, diced tomatoes, vegetable broth, thyme, and rosemary. Bring to a boil.

3. Reduce heat and simmer for 30 minutes. Stir in frozen peas and cook for an additional 15 minutes. Season with salt and pepper.

Turkey and Spinach Meatballs

Servings: 4

Cooking Time: 40 minutes

Ingredients:

- 1 lb ground turkey
- 1/2 cup breadcrumbs
- 1/2 cup grated Parmesan cheese
- 1/2 cup chopped spinach
- 1 large egg
- 2 cloves garlic, minced
- 1/2 tsp dried oregano
- Salt and pepper to taste

Instructions:

1. Preheat oven to 375°F (190°C).
2. In the mixing bowl, combine ground turkey, breadcrumbs, Parmesan cheese, spinach, egg, garlic, oregano, salt, and pepper. Mix with the paddle attachment until well combined.
3. Form mixture into meatballs and place on a baking sheet.
4. Bake for 25 minutes, until cooked through.

Baked Ziti

Servings: 6

Cooking Time: 1 hour

Ingredients:

- 1 lb ziti pasta
- 2 cups marinara sauce
- 1 cup ricotta cheese
- 1 cup shredded mozzarella cheese

- 1/2 cup grated Parmesan cheese
- 1/2 cup chopped fresh basil

Instructions:

1. Preheat oven to 375°F (190°C).
2. Cook pasta according to package instructions. Drain and set aside.
3. In a mixing bowl, combine marinara sauce, ricotta cheese, mozzarella cheese, Parmesan cheese, and basil.
4. Add cooked pasta to the bowl and mix until well coated.
5. Transfer mixture to a baking dish and bake for 30 minutes, until cheese is melted and bubbly.

Chicken Pot Pie

Servings: 6

Cooking Time: 1 hour 15 minutes

Ingredients:

Filling:

- 2 cups cooked chicken, diced
- 1 cup frozen peas and carrots
- 1/2 cup diced potatoes
- 1/4 cup all-purpose flour
- 1 cup chicken broth
- 1/2 cup milk
- 1/2 tsp dried thyme
- Salt and pepper to taste

Crust:

- 2 1/2 cups all-purpose flour
- 1/2 tsp salt
- 1 cup unsalted butter, cold and cut into cubes
- 6-8 tbsp ice water

Instructions:

1. Preheat oven to 375°F (190°C).

2. In a skillet, cook chicken, peas, carrots, and potatoes until vegetables are tender. Stir in flour and cook for 1 minute.
3. Gradually add chicken broth and milk, stirring constantly until sauce thickens. Stir in thyme, salt, and pepper.
4. For crust, combine flour and salt in the mixing bowl. Add butter and mix with the paddle attachment until mixture resembles coarse crumbs. Gradually add ice water until dough comes together.
5. Roll out dough and fit into a pie dish. Pour filling into crust.
6. Roll out remaining dough and place over filling. Trim and crimp edges to seal.
7. Bake for 40-45 minutes, until crust is golden. Let cool before serving.

Beef and Bean Chili

Servings: 6

Cooking Time: 1 hour

Ingredients:

- 1 lb ground beef
- 1 onion, chopped
- 2 cloves garlic, minced
- 1 can (14.5 oz) diced tomatoes
- 1 can (15 oz) kidney beans, drained and rinsed
- 1 can (15 oz) black beans, drained and rinsed
- 2 tbsp chili powder
- 1 tsp cumin
- 1/2 tsp paprika
- Salt and pepper to taste

Instructions:

1. In a large pot, cook ground beef, onion, and garlic until beef is browned. Drain excess fat.

2. Stir in diced tomatoes, kidney beans, black beans, chili powder, cumin, paprika, salt, and pepper.
3. Bring to a boil, then reduce heat and simmer for 30 minutes. Serve hot.

Garlic Herb Chicken Thighs

Servings: 4

Cooking Time: 45 minutes

Ingredients:

- 4 chicken thighs
- 2 tbsp olive oil
- 4 cloves garlic, minced
- 1 tbsp chopped fresh rosemary
- 1 tbsp chopped fresh thyme
- Salt and pepper to taste

Instructions:

1. Preheat oven to 400°F (200°C).
2. Rub chicken thighs with olive oil, garlic, rosemary, thyme, salt, and pepper.
3. Place chicken on a baking sheet and bake for 35-40 minutes, until cooked through and skin is crispy.

Thai Peanut Noodles

Servings: 4

Cooking Time: 30 minutes

Ingredients:

- 8 oz rice noodles
- 1/2 cup creamy peanut butter
- 1/4 cup soy sauce
- 2 tbsp honey
- 1 tbsp rice vinegar
- 1 clove garlic, minced
- 1/2 tsp grated ginger
- 1/4 cup chopped peanuts
- 2 green onions, sliced
- 1 cup shredded carrots

Instructions:

1. Cook rice noodles according to package instructions. Drain and set aside.
2. In a mixing bowl, whisk together peanut butter, soy sauce, honey, rice vinegar, garlic, and ginger until smooth.
3. Toss cooked noodles with peanut sauce until well coated.
4. Garnish with chopped peanuts, green onions, and shredded carrots.

Chapter 7: Whipping and Meringues

Master the art of whipping and creating meringues with your KitchenAid Stand Mixer. This chapter provides detailed techniques for achieving stiff peaks and light, airy textures. Learn how to use the whisk attachment effectively to elevate your desserts to a new level of perfection.

Whipping Techniques

Understanding Stiff Peaks

What Are Stiff Peaks? Stiff peaks refer to the stage when whipped egg whites or cream hold their shape and form peaks that stand upright without drooping. This consistency is essential for recipes like meringues, mousses, and whipped cream.

How to Achieve Stiff Peaks:

1. **Use the Whisk Attachment:** For optimal results, use the balloon whisk attachment, which is designed to incorporate air into the mixture efficiently.
2. Start Slow: Begin whipping on a lower speed to avoid splashing and gradually increase to high speed. This helps in creating a stable foam.
3. Clean and Dry Equipment: Ensure that your mixing bowl and whisk are completely clean and free of any grease. Even a small amount of fat can prevent the mixture from whipping properly.
4. Cold Ingredients: For whipping cream, use chilled heavy cream and a chilled mixing bowl. Cold temperatures help in achieving better volume and stability.
5. Add Stabilizers: For egg whites, adding a small amount of cream of tartar or vinegar can help stabilize the foam and prevent it from collapsing.

Technique Tips for Different Mixtures

1. **Whipping Cream:**
   Ingredients: Heavy cream, powdered sugar (optional), vanilla extract (optional).
   Procedure: Start by pouring cold heavy cream into the chilled mixing bowl. Whisk on medium speed until soft peaks form, then increase to high speed. Add powdered sugar and vanilla extract if desired, and continue whisking until stiff peaks form. Be careful not to overwhip, as it can turn into butter.
2. **Egg Whites (for Meringues):**
   Ingredients: Egg whites, granulated sugar, cream of tartar or vinegar.
   Procedure: Begin by beating egg whites and cream of tartar (or vinegar) on medium speed until foamy. Gradually add granulated sugar while increasing the speed to high. Continue to beat until stiff peaks form. This mixture should be glossy and hold its shape.
3. **Mousse and Soufflés:**
   Ingredients: Whipped cream or beaten egg whites, and other flavoring ingredients.
   Procedure: Fold whipped cream or beaten egg whites gently into other ingredients, such as chocolate or fruit purees, to maintain the airy texture. Use a rubber spatula and fold in a figure-eight motion to combine without deflating the mixture.

Whipping and Meringues Recipes

Classic Whipped Cream

Servings: 4

Cooking Time: 5 minutes

Ingredients:

- 1 cup heavy cream
- 2 tbsp powdered sugar
- 1 tsp vanilla extract

Instructions:

1. Chill the mixing bowl and whisk attachment in the freezer for 10 minutes.
2. Pour heavy cream into the chilled bowl. Add powdered sugar and vanilla extract.
3. Using the whisk attachment, beat on medium-high speed until soft peaks form.
4. Continue beating until stiff peaks form. Serve immediately or store in the refrigerator.

French Meringue

Servings: 12

Cooking Time: 1 hour (baking time)

Ingredients:

- 4 large egg whites
- 1 cup granulated sugar
- 1/4 tsp cream of tartar
- 1/2 tsp vanilla extract

Instructions:

1. Preheat oven to 225°F (110°C). Line a baking sheet with parchment paper.
2. In the mixing bowl, combine egg whites and cream of tartar. Beat on medium speed until foamy.
3. Gradually add sugar, 1 tbsp at a time, while beating on high speed until stiff peaks form.
4. Gently fold in vanilla extract.
5. Pipe or spoon meringue onto the prepared baking sheet.
6. Bake for 1 hour, until meringues are dry and crisp. Allow to cool completely before serving.

Swiss Meringue

Servings: 12

Cooking Time: 1 hour (baking time)

Ingredients:

- 4 large egg whites
- 1 cup granulated sugar
- 1/2 tsp vanilla extract

Instructions:

1. Preheat oven to 225°F (110°C). Line a baking sheet with parchment paper.
2. In a heatproof bowl, combine egg whites and sugar. Set over a pot of simmering water.
3. Whisk constantly until sugar dissolves and mixture reaches 160°F (70°C).
4. Transfer to the mixing bowl and beat on high speed until stiff peaks form and meringue is cool.
5. Gently fold in vanilla extract.
6. Pipe or spoon meringue onto the prepared baking sheet.
7. Bake for 1 hour, until meringues are dry and crisp. Allow to cool completely before serving.

Italian Meringue

Servings: 12

Cooking Time: 1 hour 15 minutes (baking time)

Ingredients:

- 4 large egg whites
- 1 cup granulated sugar
- 1/2 cup water
- 1/2 tsp vanilla extract

Instructions:

1. Preheat oven to 225°F (110°C). Line a baking sheet with parchment paper.
2. In a small saucepan, combine sugar and water. Heat over medium heat until sugar dissolves and syrup reaches 240°F (115°C).
3. In the mixing bowl, beat egg whites on medium speed until soft peaks form.
4. Gradually pour hot syrup into the egg whites while beating on high speed until stiff peaks form and mixture is cool.
5. Gently fold in vanilla extract.
6. Pipe or spoon meringue onto the prepared baking sheet.
7. Bake for 1 hour 15 minutes, until meringues are dry and crisp. Allow to cool completely before serving.

Lemon Meringue Pie

Servings: 8

Cooking Time: 1 hour 30 minutes

Ingredients:

Pie Filling:

- 1 cup granulated sugar
- 1/4 cup cornstarch
- 1 1/2 cups water
- 3 large egg yolks, lightly beaten
- 1/4 cup lemon juice
- 2 tbsp unsalted butter
- 1 tbsp lemon zest

Meringue:

- 3 large egg whites
- 1/2 tsp cream of tartar
- 1/4 cup granulated sugar

Instructions:

1. Preheat oven to 350°F (175°C). Prepare and bake pie crust according to package instructions or recipe.
2. In a saucepan, whisk together sugar and cornstarch. Gradually add water and cook over medium heat until thickened.
3. Stir a small amount of hot mixture into beaten egg yolks, then return to saucepan. Cook for 2 minutes.
4. Stir in lemon juice, butter, and lemon zest. Pour into baked pie crust.
5. For meringue, beat egg whites and cream of tartar on medium speed until foamy. Gradually add sugar while beating on high speed until stiff peaks form.
6. Spread meringue over pie filling, sealing edges.
7. Bake for 10-12 minutes, until meringue is golden. Cool before serving.

Chocolate Mousse

Servings: 6

Cooking Time: 15 minutes

Ingredients:

- 6 oz bittersweet chocolate, chopped
- 1/4 cup heavy cream
- 3 large egg whites
- 1/4 tsp cream of tartar

- 1/4 cup granulated sugar

Instructions:

1. Melt chocolate and cream in a heatproof bowl over simmering water. Stir until smooth and let cool slightly.
2. In the mixing bowl, beat egg whites and cream of tartar on medium speed until foamy. Gradually add sugar while beating on high speed until stiff peaks form.
3. Fold melted chocolate into egg whites until combined.
4. Spoon mousse into serving dishes and refrigerate for at least 2 hours before serving.

Strawberry Whipped Cream

Servings: 4

Cooking Time: 10 minutes

Ingredients:

- 1 cup heavy cream
- 1/4 cup powdered sugar
- 1/2 cup fresh strawberries, pureed

Instructions:

1. Chill the mixing bowl and whisk attachment in the freezer for 10 minutes.
2. Pour heavy cream into the chilled bowl. Add powdered sugar and strawberry puree.
3. Using the whisk attachment, beat on medium-high speed until soft peaks form.
4. Continue beating until stiff peaks form. Serve immediately or store in the refrigerator.

Pumpkin Meringue Cookies

Servings: 24

Cooking Time: 1 hour (baking time)

Ingredients:

- 3 large egg whites
- 1/2 tsp cream of tartar
- 1 cup granulated sugar
- 1/2 cup pumpkin puree
- 1 tsp pumpkin pie spice
- 1/4 tsp vanilla extract

Instructions:

1. Preheat oven to 225°F (110°C). Line a baking sheet with parchment paper.
2. In the mixing bowl, beat egg whites and cream of tartar on medium speed until foamy.
3. Gradually add sugar while beating on high speed until stiff peaks form.
4. Gently fold in pumpkin puree, pumpkin pie spice, and vanilla extract.
5. Pipe or spoon meringue onto the prepared baking sheet.
6. Bake for 1 hour, until meringues are dry and crisp. Allow to cool completely before serving.

Berry Pavlova

Servings: 6

Cooking Time: 1 hour 15 minutes

Ingredients:

Meringue:

- 4 large egg whites
- 1 cup granulated sugar

- 1/2 tsp vanilla extract
- 1/2 tsp vinegar

Topping:

- 1 cup heavy cream
- 2 tbsp powdered sugar
- 1/2 tsp vanilla extract
- 1 cup mixed fresh berries

Instructions:

1. Preheat oven to 275°F (135°C). Line a baking sheet with parchment paper.
2. In the mixing bowl, beat egg whites until soft peaks form. Gradually add sugar while beating on high speed until stiff peaks form.
3. Gently fold in vanilla extract and vinegar.
4. Spread meringue into a circular shape on the prepared baking sheet.
5. Bake for 1 hour 15 minutes, until meringue is dry and crisp. Turn off oven and let meringue cool in oven.
6. For topping, beat heavy cream, powdered sugar, and vanilla extract until soft peaks form. Spread over cooled meringue and top with fresh berries.

Cinnamon Whipped Cream

Servings: 4

Cooking Time: 5 minutes

Ingredients:

- 1 cup heavy cream
- 2 tbsp powdered sugar
- 1/2 tsp ground cinnamon

Instructions:

1. Chill the mixing bowl and whisk attachment in the freezer for 10 minutes.

2. Pour heavy cream into the chilled bowl. Add powdered sugar and ground cinnamon.
3. Using the whisk attachment, beat on medium-high speed until soft peaks form.
4. Continue beating until stiff peaks form. Serve immediately or store in the refrigerator.

Raspberry Meringue Cookies

Servings: 24

Cooking Time: 1 hour (baking time)

Ingredients:

- 3 large egg whites
- 1/2 tsp cream of tartar
- 1 cup granulated sugar
- 1/2 cup raspberry puree
- 1/4 tsp vanilla extract

Instructions:

1. Preheat oven to 225°F (110°C). Line a baking sheet with parchment paper.
2. In the mixing bowl, beat egg whites and cream of tartar on medium speed until foamy.
3. Gradually add sugar while beating on high speed until stiff peaks form.
4. Gently fold in raspberry puree and vanilla extract.
5. Pipe or spoon meringue onto the prepared baking sheet.
6. Bake for 1 hour, until meringues are dry and crisp. Allow to cool completely before serving.

Almond Meringue Cake

Servings: 8

Cooking Time: 1 hour 30 minutes

Ingredients:

Meringue Layers:
- 6 large egg whites
- 1 1/2 cups granulated sugar
- 1/2 tsp almond extract

Filling:
- 1 cup heavy cream
- 2 tbsp powdered sugar
- 1/2 tsp vanilla extract
- 1/2 cup sliced almonds

Instructions:

1. Preheat oven to 275°F (135°C). Line two baking sheets with parchment paper.
2. In the mixing bowl, beat egg whites on medium speed until foamy. Gradually add sugar while beating on high speed until stiff peaks form.
3. Gently fold in almond extract.
4. Divide meringue between prepared baking sheets, spreading into two 8-inch circles.
5. Bake for 1 hour 15 minutes, until meringues are dry and crisp. Turn off oven and let cool in oven.
6. For filling, beat heavy cream, powdered sugar, and vanilla extract until soft peaks form.
7. Place one meringue layer on a serving plate, spread with whipped cream, and sprinkle with sliced almonds. Top with second meringue layer and serve.

Mocha Meringue Nests

Servings: 12

Cooking Time: 1 hour (baking time)

Ingredients:

- 3 large egg whites
- 1/2 tsp cream of tartar
- 1 cup granulated sugar
- 2 tbsp cocoa powder
- 1 tbsp espresso powder

Instructions:

1. Preheat oven to 225°F (110°C). Line a baking sheet with parchment paper.
2. In the mixing bowl, beat egg whites and cream of tartar on medium speed until foamy.
3. Gradually add sugar while beating on high speed until stiff peaks form. Gently fold in cocoa powder and espresso powder.
4. Pipe or spoon meringue onto the prepared baking sheet, forming small nests with a well in the center.
5. Bake for 1 hour, until meringues are dry and crisp. Allow to cool completely before serving.

Mint Chocolate Meringue Bark

Servings: 16

Cooking Time: 1 hour (baking time)

Ingredients:

- 4 large egg whites
- 1 cup granulated sugar
- 1/4 tsp peppermint extract
- 1/4 cup mini chocolate chips

Instructions:

1. Preheat oven to 225°F (110°C). Line a baking sheet with parchment paper.
2. In the mixing bowl, beat egg whites on medium speed until foamy. Gradually add sugar while beating on high speed until stiff peaks form.
3. Gently fold in peppermint extract.
4. Spread meringue onto the prepared baking sheet in a thin, even layer.
5. Sprinkle mini chocolate chips over the top.
6. Bake for 1 hour, until meringue is dry and crisp. Allow to cool completely before breaking into pieces.

Chapter 8: Doughs and Batters

Perfecting Dough and Batter Consistency

Achieving the right consistency for doughs and batters is crucial for baking success. The dough hook and paddle attachment of your KitchenAid Stand Mixer can help you master this art.

Using the Dough Hook

Purpose: The dough hook is designed for kneading yeast doughs, which require a strong, consistent kneading action to develop gluten.

Technique:

1. Initial Mixing: Start on a low speed to combine ingredients without splashing.
2. Kneading: Increase to a medium speed to knead the dough. The dough should become smooth and elastic.
3. Resting: Let the dough rest and rise according to the recipe. Proper proofing is essential for dough development.

Using the Paddle Attachment

Purpose: The paddle attachment is ideal for mixing batters and doughs that do not require kneading, such as cookie doughs and cake batters.

Technique:

1. Creaming: Use the paddle to cream butter and sugar until light and fluffy.
2. Combining Ingredients: Gradually add dry ingredients to the wet mixture to avoid overmixing.
3. Mix-Ins: Add chocolate chips, nuts, or other mix-ins at low speed to distribute evenly.

Doughs and Batters Recipes

Brioche Dough

- Servings: 8 servings

- Cooking Time: 3 hours (including rising time)

Ingredients:

- 4 cups all-purpose flour

- 1/4 cup granulated sugar

- 1 tsp salt

- 1 packet active dry yeast

- 1/2 cup warm milk

- 5 large eggs

- 1 cup unsalted butter, room temperature

Instructions:

1. Combine flour, sugar, and salt in the mixer bowl.
2. Dissolve yeast in warm milk. Add to flour mixture with eggs.
3. Use the dough hook on low speed to mix until combined.
4. Increase speed to medium, adding butter gradually. Knead until dough is smooth.
5. Let dough rise until doubled in size. Shape and bake as desired.

Classic Pancake Batter

- Servings: 4 servings

- Cooking Time: 20 minutes

Ingredients:

- 1 1/2 cups all-purpose flour

- 3 1/2 tsp baking powder

- 1 tsp salt

- 1 tbsp granulated sugar

- 1 1/4 cups milk

- 1 egg

- 3 tbsp melted butter

Instructions:

1. Combine flour, baking powder, salt, and sugar in the mixer bowl.
2. Add milk, egg, and melted butter.
3. Use the paddle attachment on low speed to mix until smooth.
4. Cook on a greased griddle over medium heat until bubbles form. Flip and cook until golden.

Cinnamon Roll Dough

- Servings: 12 rolls

- Cooking Time: 2.5 hours (including rising time)

Ingredients:

- 3 1/2 cups all-purpose flour

- 1/4 cup granulated sugar

- 1 tsp salt

- 1 packet active dry yeast

- 1 cup warm milk

- 2 large eggs

- 1/3 cup unsalted butter, melted

Instructions:

1. Combine flour, sugar, and salt in the mixer bowl.

2. Dissolve yeast in warm milk. Add to flour mixture with eggs and melted butter.
3. Use the dough hook on low speed to mix until combined.
4. Increase speed to medium and knead until dough is smooth.
5. Let dough rise until doubled in size. Roll out, fill with cinnamon sugar, and bake.

Banana Bread Batter

- Servings: 1 loaf

- Cooking Time: 1 hour

Ingredients:

- 2 cups all-purpose flour
- 1 tsp baking soda
- 1/4 tsp salt
- 1/2 cup unsalted butter, room temperature
- 3/4 cup brown sugar
- 2 large eggs
- 1 tsp vanilla extract
- 2 cups mashed bananas (about 4 bananas)

Instructions:

1. Preheat oven to 350°F (175°C). Grease a loaf pan.
2. Combine flour, baking soda, and salt in the mixer bowl.
3. Cream butter and brown sugar with the paddle attachment on medium speed.
4. Add eggs and vanilla, mixing well.
5. Add mashed bananas and mix until combined.
6. Gradually add dry ingredients. Mix until just combined.
7. Pour batter into the loaf pan and bake for 60 minutes or until a toothpick comes out clean.

Pizza Dough

- Servings: 2 pizzas
- Cooking Time: 1.5 hours (including rising time)

Ingredients:

- 3 1/2 cups all-purpose flour

- 1 tsp salt

- 1 packet active dry yeast

- 1 1/2 cups warm water

- 2 tbsp olive oil

Instructions:

1. Combine flour and salt in the mixer bowl.
2. Dissolve yeast in warm water. Add to flour mixture with olive oil.
3. Use the dough hook on low speed to mix until combined.
4. Increase speed to medium and knead until dough is smooth and elastic.
5. Let dough rise until doubled in size. Roll out and add toppings. Bake at 475°F (245°C) for 12-15 minutes.

Blueberry Muffin Batter

- Servings: 12 muffins

- Cooking Time: 25 minutes

Ingredients:

- 2 cups all-purpose flour

- 1/2 cup granulated sugar

- 1/2 cup brown sugar

- 1 tsp baking powder

- 1/2 tsp baking soda

- 1/2 tsp salt

- 1 cup buttermilk

- 1/2 cup vegetable oil

- 2 large eggs

- 1 tsp vanilla extract

- 1 cup blueberries

Instructions:

1. Preheat oven to 375°F (190°C). Line a muffin tin with paper liners.
2. Combine flour, sugars, baking powder, baking soda, and salt in the mixer bowl.
3. In a separate bowl, whisk together buttermilk, oil, eggs, and vanilla.
4. Use the paddle attachment on low speed to combine dry and wet ingredients until just mixed.
5. Gently fold in blueberries.
6. Divide batter among muffin cups and bake for 20-25 minutes until golden brown.

Scone Dough

- Servings: 8 scones

- Cooking Time: 30 minutes

Ingredients:

- 2 cups all-purpose flour
- 1/3 cup granulated sugar
- 1 tbsp baking powder
- 1/2 tsp salt
- 1/2 cup cold unsalted butter, cut into pieces
- 1/2 cup heavy cream
- 1 large egg
- 1 tsp vanilla extract
- **Optional:** 1 cup add-ins (berries, chocolate chips, etc.)

Instructions:

1. Preheat oven to 400°F (200°C). Line a baking sheet with parchment paper.
2. Combine flour, sugar, baking powder, and salt in the mixer bowl.
3. Add cold butter and mix with the paddle attachment until the mixture resembles coarse crumbs.
4. In a separate bowl, whisk together cream, egg, and vanilla.
5. Gradually add wet ingredients to dry ingredients. Mix until just combined.
6. Fold in add-ins if using.
7. Turn dough onto a floured surface, shape into a disk, and cut into wedges. Bake for 15-20 minutes until golden brown.

Waffle Batter

- Servings: 4 servings

- Cooking Time: 20 minutes

Ingredients:

- 2 cups all-purpose flour

- 2 tbsp granulated sugar

- 1 tbsp baking powder

- 1/2 tsp salt

- 2 large eggs

- 1 3/4 cups milk

- 1/2 cup vegetable oil

- 1 tsp vanilla extract

Instructions:

1. Preheat waffle iron.
2. Combine flour, sugar, baking powder, and salt in the mixer bowl.
3. In a separate bowl, whisk together eggs, milk, oil, and vanilla.

4. Use the paddle attachment on low speed to combine dry and wet ingredients until smooth.
5. Pour batter into preheated waffle iron and cook until golden brown.

Pumpkin Bread Batter

• Servings: 1 loaf

• Cooking Time: 1 hour

Ingredients:

• 1 3/4 cups all-purpose flour

• 1 tsp baking soda

• 1/2 tsp salt

• 1/2 tsp ground cinnamon

• 1/2 tsp ground nutmeg

• 1/4 tsp ground cloves

• 1/4 tsp ground ginger

• 1 cup granulated sugar

• 1/2 cup vegetable oil

• 2 large eggs

• 1 cup pumpkin puree

Instructions:

1. Preheat oven to 350°F (175°C). Grease a loaf pan.
2. Combine flour, baking soda, salt, and spices in the mixer bowl.
3. In a separate bowl, whisk together sugar, oil, eggs, and pumpkin puree.
4. Use the paddle attachment on low speed to combine dry and wet ingredients until smooth.
5. Pour batter into the loaf pan and bake for 60 minutes or until a toothpick comes out clean.

Cornbread Batter

• Servings: 8 servings

• Cooking Time: 25 minutes

Ingredients:

• 1 cup cornmeal

• 1 cup all-purpose flour

• 1/4 cup granulated sugar

• 1 tbsp baking powder

• 1/2 tsp salt

• 1 cup milk

• 1/4 cup vegetable oil

• 2 large eggs

Instructions:

1. Preheat oven to 400°F (200°C). Grease a baking dish.
2. Combine cornmeal, flour, sugar, baking powder, and salt in the mixer bowl.
3. In a separate bowl, whisk together milk, oil, and eggs.
4. Use the paddle attachment on low speed to combine dry and wet ingredients until smooth.
5. Pour batter into the baking dish and bake for 20-25 minutes until golden brown.

Crepe Batter

• Servings: 4 servings

• Cooking Time: 15 minutes

Ingredients:

• 1 cup all-purpose flour

• 2 large eggs

• 1/2 cup milk

- 1/2 cup water

- 1/4 tsp salt

- 2 tbsp melted butter

Instructions:

1. Combine all ingredients in the mixer bowl.
2. Use the paddle attachment on low speed to mix until smooth.
3. Heat a lightly oiled griddle or frying pan over medium-high heat.
4. Pour or scoop the batter onto the griddle, using approximately 1/4 cup for each crepe. Cook until lightly browned on both sides.

Chocolate Chip Cookie Dough

- Servings: 24 cookies

- Cooking Time: 15 minutes

Ingredients:

- 2 1/4 cups all-purpose flour

- 1 tsp baking soda

- 1/2 tsp salt

- 1 cup unsalted butter, room temperature

- 3/4 cup granulated sugar

- 3/4 cup brown sugar

- 1 tsp vanilla extract

- 2 large eggs

- 2 cups chocolate chips

Instructions:

1. Preheat oven to 375°F (190°C). Line a baking sheet with parchment paper.
2. Combine flour, baking soda, and salt in the mixer bowl.

3. Cream butter and sugars with the paddle attachment on medium speed.
4. Add vanilla and eggs, one at a time, mixing well after each addition.
5. Gradually add dry ingredients. Mix until just combined.
6. Fold in chocolate chips.
7. Drop by rounded tablespoons onto the baking sheet and bake for 10-12 minutes until golden brown.

Conclusion

Embrace the Versatility of Your Stand Mixer

Congratulations on completing your journey through the world of baking and cooking with your KitchenAid Stand Mixer! Whether you're crafting delicate pastries, hearty breads, or savory dishes, this versatile tool has proven to be an invaluable companion in your kitchen.

Key Takeaways

1. **Mastery of Techniques:** From achieving the perfect dough consistency for cookies to creating light and fluffy cakes, your stand mixer's attachments—paddle, dough hook, and whisk—are designed to help you achieve professional results with ease.
2. **Recipes for Every Occasion:** You now have a diverse collection of recipes at your fingertips. Each one has been crafted to showcase the full potential of your stand mixer, ensuring you can create delicious and impressive dishes for any occasion.
3. **Efficient Cooking and Baking:** The stand mixer's power and precision simplify the cooking process, saving you time and effort while enhancing the consistency and quality of your baked goods and savory dishes.

Measurement Conversions

Measure	Fluid OZ	TBSP	tsp	Liter (l) Milliliter (ml)
1 gallon	4 quarts	256 tbsp	768 tsp	3.1 l
4 cups	1 quart	64 tbsp	192 tsp	0.95 l
2 cups	1 pint	32 tbsp	96 tsp	470 ml
1 cup	8 oz	16 tbsp	48 tsp	237 ml
3/4 cup	6 oz	12 tbsp	36 tsp	177 ml
2/3 cup	5 oz	11 tbsp	32 tsp	158 ml
1/2 cup	4 oz	8 tbsp	24 tsp	118 ml
1/3 cup	3 oz	5 tbsp	16 tsp	79 ml
1/4 cup	2 oz	4 tbsp	12 tsp	59 ml
1/8 cup	1 oz	2 tbsp	6 tsp	30 ml
1/16 cup	0.5 oz	1 tbsp	3 tsp	15 ml

About the Author

Eloise Ford

With a passion for both culinary arts and the science of baking, Eloise is a dedicated food writer and culinary expert. Combining years of experience in professional kitchens with a deep love for home cooking, She brings a wealth of knowledge and creativity to the world of food.

Eloise is particularly enthusiastic about KitchenAid Stand Mixers, recognizing them as essential tools in both professional and home kitchens. Their extensive use and understanding of this versatile appliance have inspired the creation of this comprehensive recipe book, aimed at helping others unlock the full potential of their stand mixers.

Recipe Index

A

Almond Croissants, *44*
Almond Meringue Cake, *66*

B

Bagels, *16*
Baked Ziti, *57*
Banana Bread Batter, *71*
BBQ Pulled Pork, *56*
Beef and Broccoli Stir-Fry, *55*
Berry Pavlova, *64*
Blueberry Hand Pies, *42*
Blueberry Muffin Batter, *71*
Black Forest Cake, *27*
Blondies, *35*
Brioche, *13*
Brioche Dough, *70*
Brownies, *35*
Banana Cupcakes, *24*
Beef and Bean Chili, *58*

C

Chicken Enchiladas, *54*
Chicken Parmesan, *52*
Chocolate Cupcakes, *22*
Chocolate Mousse, *63*
Challah, *17*
Chicken Pot Pie, *58*
Chocolate Chip Cookie Dough, *74*
Chocolate Cream Pie, *47*
Chocolate Eclairs, *43*
Chocolate Lava Cakes, *26*
Chocolate Mint Tart, *48*
Ciabatta, *15*
Cinnamon Rolls, *16*
Cinnamon Whipped Cream, *65*
Classic Chocolate Chip Cookies, *32*
Classic Meatloaf, *52*
Classic White Bread, *12*
Classic Apple Pie, *41*
Classic Beef Stroganoff, *52*
Classic Pancake Batter, *70*
Classic Vanilla Cake, *22*
Classic Whipped Cream, *62*
Coconut Cake, *25*
Coconut Macaroons, *36*
Creamy Chicken and Spinach Pasta, *53*

Crepe Batter, *73*
Carrot Cake, *24*
Cinnamon Roll Dough, *70*
Cornbread Batter, *73*

D

Double Chocolate Chip Cookies, *34*

E

English Muffins, *18*

F

French Meringue, *62*
French Baguette, *13*
Focaccia, *14*

G

Garlic Herb Chicken Thighs, *59*
Ginger Molasses Cookies, *38*

I

Italian Meringue, *63*

L

Lemon Bars, *34*
Lemon Meringue Pie, *41*
Lemon Meringue Pie, *63*
Lemon Pound Cake, *23*
Lentil and Vegetable Stew, *57*

M

Mint Chocolate Meringue Bark, *66*
Mocha Meringue Nests, *66*
Marble Cake, *25*

N

Naan, *18*

O

Oatmeal Raisin Cookies, *32*
Orange Chiffon Cake, *26*

P

Peach Galette, *45*
Peanut Butter Cookies, *33*
Pecan Pie, *46*
Pita Bread, *15*
Pretzels, *19*
Pumpkin Spice Cupcakes, *28*
Pumpkin Bread Batter, *73*
Pumpkin Meringue Cookies, *64*
Pumpkin Pie, *43*
Pear Almond Tart, *48*

Pineapple Upside-Down Cake, *28*
Pizza Dough, *71*

Q

Quiche Lorraine, *44*

R

Raspberry Almond Tart, *49*
Raspberry Bars, *35*
Raspberry Almond Bars, *38*
Raspberry Meringue Cookies, *65*
Red Velvet Cake, *23*
Rye Bread, *14*

S

S'mores Bars, *36*
Shrimp and Grits, *56*
Snickerdoodle Cookies, *33*
Spinach and Ricotta Stuffed Shells, *55*
Strawberry Rhubarb Pie, *45*
Strawberry Shortcake, *27*

Strawberry Whipped Cream, *64*
Stuffed Bell Peppers, *56*
Swiss Meringue, *62*
Salted Caramel Bars, *37*
Savory Beef and Vegetable Pie, *54*
Sourdough Bread, *13*
Spicy Sausage and Pepper Skillet, *53*
Scone Dough, *72*

T

Thai Peanut Noodles, *59*
Turkey Meatballs in Tomato Sauce, *54*
Turkey and Spinach Meatballs, *57*
Tarts aux Pommes, *46*
Tiramisu Cupcakes, *29*

W

Whole Wheat Bread, *12*
White Chocolate Cranberry Cookies, *37*
Waffle Batter, *72*

Made in the USA
Coppell, TX
17 December 2024

42987942R00044